Detecting Regime Change in Computational Finance

Detecting Regime Change in Computational Finance

Data Science, Machine Learning and Algorithmic Trading

Jun Chen
Edward P K Tsang

CRC Press
Taylor & Francis Group
Boca Raton London New York

CRC Press is an imprint of the
Taylor & Francis Group, an **informa** business

A CHAPMAN & HALL BOOK

First edition published 2021
by CRC Press
6000 Broken Sound Parkway NW, Suite 300, Boca Raton, FL 33487-2742

and by CRC Press
2 Park Square, Milton Park, Abingdon, Oxon, OX14 4RN

© 2021 Jun Chen and Edward P K Tsang

CRC Press is an imprint of Taylor & Francis Group, LLC

ISBN: 978-0-367-53628-2 (hbk)
ISBN: 978-0-367-54095-1 (pbk)
ISBN: 978-1-003-08759-5 (ebk)

Contents

Appendices

Foreword

The book *Detecting Regime Change in Computational Finance* is the first book of its kind to build on the framework of Directional Change. The concept of Directional Change is a new field of research that rethinks the way in which data is represented and sampled. The methodology opens a whole new area of research, which raises fundamental questions about model-design and proposes an alternative approach to it. Instead of sampling data according to the pulse of physical time, the new methodology uses the Directional Change operator to filter the data and pick out the truly relevant data points. The new approach was developed because established methodologies have not rendered satisfactory results and are not fulfilling expectations. Market prices are not recorded at fixed intervals and time does not flow at the same pace during the course of 24 hours and over a week, where different time periods are not equally meaningful. The Directional Change framework is a methodology to select the time points that are significant.

I am deeply grateful for the many years of friendship and support of Professor Edward Tsang of the Centre for Computational Finance and Economic Agents, Essex University. We had a great working relationship! Thank you, Edward, for sharing your enthusiasm with the students, and encouraging them to explore the new framework, and to dig deeper to achieve a better understanding of the benefits of the new approach. Many thanks to you, Jun Chen, for embarking on an exciting research project and making your work accessible in a book.

The great technological innovations in natural sciences in the last century were possible because the scientists were data driven and ready to embrace new theories. This openness led to the development of computers, the Internet technology and mobile telephony. Technological innovation has had a transformative impact on modern society that can be experienced day by day. The ability to make telephone calls with a mobile from anywhere in the world, is just one example of a technical feat that was inconceivable only 50 years ago. Scientific progress in social sciences did not match the progress made in natural sciences. The disappointing performance of social sciences is painfully obvious in the many shortcomings of the modern economy and the fallout of the Coronavirus pandemic. The depletion of natural resources and the evermore threatening news of global warming are additional evidence of the failure of the economic system to allocate resources in a sustainable way, as well as the lack of progress in social sciences.

The catalyst for progress in natural science is the data-centric methodology that has led to unexpected discoveries. The Michelson–Morley experiment conducted in 1887, which paved the way for the discovery of the theory of relativity illustrates how data-driven natural scientists are, as one example. At a time when technology was in its infancy and exact measurements were extremely difficult, the physicists Albert. A. Michelson and Edward W. Morley went about measuring the speed of light in different directions. The outcome of the Michelson–Morley experiment was a big surprise. The results showed beyond doubt that the speed of light is a constant and invariant.

This discovery debunked existing theories. Scientists were open to accept defeat and ready to question their basic assumptions. Their openness paved the way for the discovery of relativity theory and, indirectly, quantum theory.

The Michelson–Morley experiment is an example of the benefits of a data-centric research methodology and the necessity of putting in established theories when empirical evidence does not align with the inferences of existing theories. We need to embrace new theories even though they may challenge existing assumptions that are deeply ingrained in the public perception.

I was first introduced to the deficiencies of economic theories while studying at Oxford in 1980. James Mirrlees [1], who would later receive a Nobel Prize in economics, explained in an economics class that established growth models were unsatisfactory and did not answer the real problem. I still hear his words explaining that growth models derail if one screwdriver breaks and is unstable. This was deeply troubling. If growth models cannot account for machines breaking down, or other things going wrong, then these models miss out on an essential feature of economic and social progress. The history of humankind has one constant: things go wrong and unexpected negative events are a daily occurrence. Wars and human errors are omnipresent. Economic

---

[1]See https://en.wikipedia.org/wiki/James_Mirrlees

theory has to account for and be able to incorporate setbacks into its modelling framework.

Encouraged by the intellectual openness of the Oxford academic environment, I started a long journey of investigation and research, going back to the first principles of economics in search of a more stable model framework. In the process, I started to develop a relativistic framework that I called *system theory* to explain economic phenomena. On my journey of developing a new theory, I started to investigate the nature of time and its definition, and eventually realised that there are some very basic open questions.

Economic and finance models use historical data as inputs to test and validate the models. The validation process is an essential stepping-stone in model building. It is there that basic questions can arise. Take a simple example of computing the price average of the EUR vs. the USD since the beginning of the year. How should the data be sampled? Should prices be sampled every day, including Saturdays and Sundays, or only on weekdays? How should public holidays such as Christmas and Easter be dealt with? How should one account for the holiday schedules of the different countries? At what time of the day should the data be sampled? What frequency of sampling is appropriate? How should one deal with intra-day price data? Should the researcher include in the computation every price recorded, or restrict the analysis to a fixed time interval of minutes or hours? Some financial instruments are traded very actively and have price updates every second or more, whereas other instruments are traded infrequently and have only a few updates per day. The end result of the computation depends on the specific decision of how to sample data.

It is necessary to differentiate between the data points that the researcher has collected, and the data is sampled for the computation of the price average in this case. The sampled data series is not a strict mapping of the physical time scale; it is based on another time scale defined by the researcher, who decided on how to sample the data series and set the specific details of the definition of time in this particular context. The different definitions of time can be an issue of concern, when comparing results between researchers and types of investigations. The Michelson–Morley experiment of 1887 illustrates the benefits of meticulous work to achieve progress. The mismatch between physical time scale and actual time scale mentioned above is no trivial matter. It is only after many years that I understood its full significance and why this issue needs to be addressed to make significant progress in economics.

After Oxford, I did a PhD in law at the University of Zurich, and the title of my thesis was 'Interaction between Law and Society'. My thesis was far ranging and included an outline for a new economic theory inspired by relativity theory. It is in this context that the initial idea of intrinsic time developed, which ultimately developed into the Directional Change operator. After my PhD, I joined a bank to combine academic and practical work in the hope to be more productive than in a purely academic setting. I started as a lawyer, then joined the research team, and finally worked as a trader in the foreign exchange department. Frustrated by the lack of innovation at the bank, I launched a startup in 1985 with the name of Olsen & Associates, Research Institute for Applied Economics, in Zurich, little knowing the obstacles that I would encounter. Setting up a company was the start of a big adventure that is continuing to this day with my newest venture called Lykke, a blockchain company. I have been spoiled by the unique support of my parents and my close family. During all these years, I have worked with highly gifted and dedicated colleagues who have made decisive contributions. It is only thanks to their help that we have made progress and succeeded; a big thank you to all!

At Olsen & Associates in 1985, we started to build an information system using BigData with real–time forecasts and trading recommendations with a graphical user interface. After many setbacks, we acquired 60 top institutions across Europe as customers. Our service included foreign exchange and fixed-income markets. We did not have the resources to expand into equities and other markets, which was a pity.

In 1995, we had a major highlight. We organised the first high-frequency finance conference. We made available a data set of 117 micro market maker quotes of foreign exchange markets to researchers around the world. Access to a data set of this size was a novelty and contributed to the development of market microstructure as a new discipline in economics. Over the years, we were confronted with many obstacles in developing real–time decision support services, and this led to the publication of many scientific and working papers.

In 1999, Ramo Gençay, an economist from Canada, joined Olsen & Associates as a visiting scholar during his sabbatical. Ramo was fascinated by the insights that we had accumulated about modelling financial markets. Thanks to his energy and enthusiasm we were able to publish the book *An Introduction to High-Frequency Finance* [2]. The book explains how tick-by-tick market data can be used to model financial markets, to generate volatility and price forecasts and to build trading models. The book rapidly became required reading for quantitative hedge funds. Tragically, in 2017, Ramo passed away and therefore was not part of our plan of organising a conference about time. The Directional Change framework would have been a key topic. Ramo had a unique integrity and openness to new ideas; a big thank you for his friendship and the great time that we spent together.

The high-frequency finance book was a big achievement, but I was disappointed, as I had not reached my goal. Our methods and tools were better than standard Excel-type spreadsheet models by a margin of 20 to 30%. They were not an order of magnitude better to aid understanding, and financial markets continued to be an opaque, unfathomable monster. Major breakthroughs in natural sciences imply an improvement of an order of magnitude; our methods and tools clearly did not achieve this goal. Personally, I had assembled a lot of small pieces of evidence that a breakthrough would be possible but could not connect the dots. I decided to go back to the drawing board. I was lucky and unlucky at the same time.

When the book was published in 2001, the dot-com bubble burst. Olsen & Associates had been struggling financially and had lots of valuable products but did not have the necessary distribution power. It was only at the very end of the dot-com boom in 2000 that we succeeded in getting traction from investment bankers and organised a funding round. The bubble burst before the funding was closed, and we were on the dry with no other funding sources. The company went into default. Luckily, OANDA, the Internet spinoff of Olsen & Associates, survived. The company was independent and launched its new FX trading platform, offering second-by-second interest payments and allowing small and big traders to transact at the same spread. This was a novelty in the industry. The platform was an instant success, and OANDA turned into a shooting star.

The trading platform soon had several tens of thousands of users and was a unique research laboratory to study trader behaviour and

---

[2]Dacorogna, Michel M., Gençay, Ramazan., Müller, Ulrich., Olsen, Richard B., & Olivier V, Pictet. (2001). *An Introduction to High-Frequency Finance*, Academic Press.

market mechanisms from first-hand experience. It increased my awareness of how path-dependent the price trajectory of financial markets is. On one occasion, there was a young trader of 24 years who had received tens of millions from his father and opened a position of one billion. The trader did not know how to trade in a responsible way, and a margin call could have tipped the global FX market. There are many more stories of how path-dependent market prices are, and how the flapping of butterflies can change the trajectory of markets.

Olsen & Associates and its other entities were restructured in 2001 and transformed into a small asset management company focused on foreign exchange. I had decided to just focus on trading model development for the most efficient financial market of all, foreign exchange. Algorithmic trading models are statistical operators that model the process of the respective financial instrument; for example, the EUR/USD exchange rate. The profitability of trading models is a measure of the quality of the underlying models. My goal was to build profitable trading models for the most efficient market of the world, the foreign exchange market, with today over 6.5 trillion USD of daily turnover [3]. We started our work by stripping the existing trading models to their bare bones, trying to figure out in detail what drives the profitability of trading models.

During the course of this work, a fundamental and philosophical question came up that I initially had investigated in my dissertation in the context of relativity theory and economics: does an absolute frame of reference exist? Relativity theory has gone beyond the framework of classical physics and its one system assumption, and opened the question of what happens when there are different systems that move at different speeds. I expanded that thought and considered what happens when different systems meet each other again. In the famous twin example of relativity theory, the twins can grow older at different rates, depending on their speed. What happens when the two twins of different ages meet each other again? I interpreted every trader as a system in his own right and started to think how information travels between traders and the market as a whole.

Every trader is a system on its own that is moving through space at different speeds. The trader experiences his or her flow of time as a function of profitability. When a trader makes a lot of money, then this feels like moving through space like a rocket. When a trader loses money,

---

[3]See https://www.bis.org/statistics/rpfx19_fx.pdf

the pain level increases and time slows down. The trader watches the price screen second-by-second, giving him the sensation that the flow of time is coming to a standstill. Traders view market events very differently depending on their position. A price jump of one percent within a minute that occurs immediately after opening a new position is a big acceleration for one trader, and he has the feeling of a rapidly accelerating car. Another trader in the same dealing room, who opened his position a long time ago and sits on a loss of a few percent, for him the same price bounce is just a minor price reversal that hardly registers in his brain. The big question was, 'How to translate this descriptive language of how time flows for a trader into operational tools that can be tested in the market and implemented in our trading models?'

From the very start of our research at Olsen & Associates, inspired by my PhD work, we had tried to move away from physical time and apply the concept of intrinsic time to improve the quality of our models. We used a volatility weighting scheme based on the absolute price scaling laws [4] to rescale time. During periods of high volatility, the model would lengthen time duration; and during periods of low volatility time, durations would be compressed. The model results were significantly better, but not more than that. We did not understand why. In the years after 2001, I wanted to get to the bottom of the problem and develop a bare-bone trading model to understand what drives performance. In the process, we rediscovered the directional time operator that was first discussed in the paper of 1997, where we presented an overview of the key statistical properties of foreign exchange markets [5], [6]. We explained that the average frequency of Directional Changes of different sizes follows a scaling law. This was surprising to us, but we failed to fully appreciate the significance of this result. We did not realise that the Directional Change operator would lead to the discovery of many more scaling laws and, ultimately, a new approach to economic model building and more. We achieved this breakthrough

---

[4]See Müller, U., et al. (1990). Statistical study of foreign exchange rates, empirical evidence of a price change scaling law, and intraday analysis, *Journal of Banking & Finance*, 14(6), 1189–1208, https://www.sciencedirect.com/science/article/abs/pii/037842669090009

[5]See 'From the bird's eye to the microscope: A survey of new stylized facts of the intra-daily foreign exchange market', published in 1997

[6]See https://link.springer.com/article/10.1007/s007800050018

in 2008 [7]. Thanks to the painstaking work of James Glattfelder, we discovered that the Directional Change operator identifies statistical properties of financial time series that had remained hidden.

The Directional Change operator picks up information about price extremes and reversals. The price extremes are important, because margin calls and limit orders are conditional to the price extremes recorded. They dictate if a margin call or limit order is executed or not. This impacts the p/l of a trader or any algorithm. If a limit order is hit and a trader can open his position, he can benefit from a subsequent price move. If the limit order is not met, then his position is not opened. Vice versa, if a margin call gets triggered, a trader is kicked out of his position and is forced to realise a loss and cannot recoup his losses from the subsequent price move. The Directional Change operator picks up information that is critical for how the price trajectory of the market unfolds and how the intrinsic time of the individual traders' ticks. The operator can be used with different thresholds to investigate market conditions at different scales. The remarkable feature is that the observed properties are fractal and there exists a wealth of different scaling laws. The Glattfelder paper is an initial set of scaling laws and many more are there to be explored.

From 2008 onwards, it took us many years to consolidate our discovery and understand how to leverage it for trading model algorithms. In 2017, we published the paper 'The Alpha Engine: Designing an Automated Trading Algorithm', [8] with an overview of our approach. The work of developing automated trading algorithms has just begun, and there is a big world to explore. This book *Detecting Regime Change in Computational Finance*, is an important step towards improving our understanding of the framework of Directional Change and building decision support tools. My sincere thanks to Edward Tsang, Jun Chen and the publishers for contributing to this new field of research!

Richard Olsen

---

[7]See J.B. Glattfelder et al, Patterns in high-frequency FX data: Discovery of 12 empirical scaling laws, https://arxiv.org/abs/0809.1040

[8]Golub, A, et al. (2017). The Alpha Engine: Designing an Automated Trading Algorithm. In *High-Performance Computing in Finance* (pp.49–76). Chapman and Hall/CRC. https://papers.ssrn.com/sol3/papers.cfm?abstract_id=2951348

Preface

Our book is an attempt to push forward in the field of financial analysis, using new ways to engage with financial data, under our chosen method of Directional Change, and harnessing some of the cutting-edge tools of machine learning and the related algorithmic trading.

One of the questions we had to frame was, 'what is time?'. Einstein suggested that 'Time has no independent existence apart from the order of events by which we measure it' (*The Universe & Dr Einstein by Lincoln Barnett*). If no one buys and sells in the market, or the price never changes, whether one takes a daily, hourly or minute approach, time series as a concept does not matter. Time series is only useful if it records price changes. And if that is the case, then why don't we simply record only significant price changes in the market? That is the basic concept behind Directional Change – that – only significant price movements are recorded – and that is the framework that this work is built on.

The idea of Directional Change was known as 'zigzag' in technical analysis, because of the pattern it made. Thus, this book does cover aspects of technical analysis. But the approach taken in this book does not make assumptions about trading behaviour in the market. It is solely a data-driven approach: it lets the data tell us what is happening in the market and also indicates the importance of external events to market operation, for the market does not exist in isolation.

The authors have been privileged to have learned about the concept of Directional Change through the pioneering work of Richard Olsen. In high-frequency finance and in Directional Change, Olsen is decades ahead of his time. We are grateful to him for writing for this book such a fascinating Foreword, explaining some of the complexities of Directional Change that have fascinated him. It was Richard Olsen who recognized Mandelbrot's fractal characteristics of directional changes: that some properties remain constant when the market is observed under different scales. Although the concept of zigzag existed in technical analysis, it has never before been studied as a scientific, data-centric concept, as Olsen and we have attempted to do.

'Knowledge is power', said Elizabethan philosopher Sir Francis Bacon. Data scientists believe that knowledge can be acquired through information, where information can be extracted from data. Directional Change provides an alternative view to financial data, and, as Richard Olsen has pointed out in his Foreword, it provides an alternative way to extract information from it. The most significant finding was probably the power laws discovered by Olsen and his team, which could not have been observed under time series.

This book is also about machine learning and algorithmic trading. Machine learning attempts to find regularities in the market. Such regularities would only help trading if they persisted in the market. However, sometimes the traders collectively behave differently; this is known as *regime change* in the market. When that happens, traders must be able to react accordingly; for example, by closing their positions. For example, data suggests that the regime changed in the currency market around the time when the Brexit referendum took place in the UK. This book proposes an effective direction towards monitoring regime changes in the market.

The authors have also benefited from interaction with many collaborators; in particular, Alex Dupuis, Raju Venkata Chinthalapati, Antoaneta Serguieva, Wing Lon Ng, Steve Phelps, John O'Hara, David Norman, Michael Kampouridis, Yi Cao, Shaimaa Masry, Monira Aloud, Ao Han, Amer Bakhach, Hamid Jalalian, Tao Ran, Chen Chen, Ma Shuai, Alan Ye, Gao Jing, Shengnan Li, and Shicheng Hu. In fact, all the students that we have taught have helped to sharpen our concept on this topic. We are also grateful to Michael Lung, Fay Somerville and Huiling Liu who brought this team together. We would like to express our special thanks to Sara Colquhoun, who started as our English coach but, through dedication and studiousness, has since made herself an expert in Directional Change.

Our work owes much to our colleagues in this field, and we very much hope we have added to the field of research as well.

Jun Chen
Edward P K Tsang
Spring 2020

List of Figures

List of Tables

CHAPTER 1

Introduction

1.1 OVERVIEW

T HIS book is about data analysis in finance. What useful information could one extract from data? To allow us to go into great depth in this book, we focus on information about regime changes, which means changes in the collective behaviour of the traders in the market. Being able to recognize regime changes in the market is important for traders and regulators. This book starts by asking "what are the data telling us about the market". Then it explains how the information extracted from the data could help us monitor the market, to see whether it has entered a different regime. Then, as a proof of concept, it explains how a trader could benefit from such information. We shall explain that both knowledge representation and machine learning (two important branches of Artificial Intelligence (AI)) play important roles in information extraction.

How one represents knowledge determines how one could reason about it. Instead of using time series to summarise price changes in the market, this book takes the Directional Change (DC) approach. In time series, one samples a transaction price at fixed intervals, for example, daily closing prices. Directional change is a data-driven approach. It lets data tell us when to sample a transaction price. This will be explained in details in Chapter 2. By looking at price changes from a different angle, we are able to extract new information from data. Such new information complements what we observe under time series. We shall show that being able to see with two eyes (time series and directional change) is better than seeing with one (time series alone).

We cannot observe the individual trader's behaviour, but the price dynamics in the market reflects their collective behaviour. Statistical properties of the price dynamics is observable. With machine learning, we could use the price dynamics to estimate the hidden processes that drive the market into different regimes. We can also use past observations to statistically estimate whether the market is going to change from one regime to another. Such estimations give traders a chance to adjust their trading strategies. By nature of the directional change definition, the market can be monitored tick-by-tick. This makes the proposed method particularly suitable for high-frequency finance [20].

This book should be seen as a proof of concept. It shows that data does not have to be sampled at fixed intervals (as in time series). Data can be sampled based on events (directional changes). It shows that machine learning can be used to find hidden models in data. It shows that markets can be monitored to detect regime changes. It shows that regime information can help algorithmic trading. It demonstrates a new research framework, a framework in which more effective market monitoring methods, more effective machine learning methods, more effective algorithmic trading algorithms can be applied.

1.2 RESEARCH OBJECTIVES

The aim of this study is to identify and measure the underlying trend of regime change in the financial market, so as to create a practical and theoretical framework to monitor the financial markets. This study aims to answer the following four research questions:

1. Traditionally, most research on regime change starts with summarising data as time series. In this book, we wanted to see if regime change can also be detected under the framework of DC. Therefore, we proposed a new methodology to detect regime change with a data summary under DC in Chapter 3.

2. As a DC-based regime change detection method is proposed, a number of further questions are raised. For example, would regime change detected under DC be the same as regime change detected under time series? Or would they be different? We then focus on evaluating the effectiveness of these two approaches (DC and time series) on regime change detection, in our first research chapter, Chapter 3.

3. Once regime changes can be effectively detected under the data-driven approach of DC, our next aim is to see what classifications or taxonomy can then be applied to regime change. One possible option is to characterise "normal market regime" and "abnormal market regime" in financial markets. The aim is to cover different markets, different periods and different data types, to see whether they share anything in common, which can be used as the factors that determine the market into the two categories. This topic is discussed in our second research chapter, Chapter 4.

4. Leading on from research to establish the parameters for normal and abnormal regimes through the mechanism of DC, the next aim is to take an in-depth look at what leads to the shift from one market regime to another. The aim is to track the financial market to see whether it is entering into one regime from another. In particular, whether the market is shifting to an abnormally volatile regime from a normal, less volatile regime. This would allow us to monitor the status of the financial market in real time, under our specially developed DC analysis and machine learning techniques. And, as a further move, this study could lay the foundation for establishing a practical financial early warning system.

5. Being able to track regime changes allows us to know the current status of the financial market. The early warning signals of regime changes allow investors to better understand the market. However, we wonder if this information would be useful for practical trading. One way to find out is to develop trading algorithms based on the regime tracking signals. By comparing the performance of the designed trading algorithms, we should find the impact of regime tracking information on practical trading.

In summary, our fundamental research objective is therefore to establish a methodology of regime change recognition, and to be able to go on to classify different types of market regimes and dynamically track regime changes under DC, as an alternative way to understand the operation of the financial market and its characteristics. Lastly, we attempt to establish practical trading algorithms based on the regime tracking information.

1.3 BOOK STRUCTURE

This book is organised as follows:

In Chapter 2, we begin with reviewing the principal current research and literature on regime change. Besides, this chapter also provides a general overview of the concept of Directional Change and its application. Lastly, the relevant machine learning techniques, which are adopted in this book, are outlined.

In Chapter 3, we propose a new methodology to detect regime changes in financial markets based on Directional Change. The proposed method is then compared with the conventional approach in regime change detection.

In Chapter 4, we extend our analysis of regime changes detection to classify different market regimes. In particular, we attempt to characterise what is a "normal market regime" as well as an "abnormal market regime". In the empirical study, we investigate regime changes in ten different financial markets and then classify the market regimes that occur.

In the next research chapter, Chapter 5, we examine the features of what makes up the bridge, or movement, between different market regimes, and indicate the possibility of constructing a programme to monitor the financial markets in real time, so as to be able to track what is the current regime in the financial markets.

In Chapter 6, we propose two simple trading algorithms, which make use of the regime tracking information that is generated by the method presented in Chapter 5. By comparing the performance of the designed trading algorithms, we demonstrate the usefulness of the tracking signals for practical trading.

Thus, the four research chapters are proposed to be a programme of new theoretical and empirical research on the topic of regime change, with, for the first time, the examination to be carried out using Directional Change, a data-driven approach, and examining and testing for the strengths and weaknesses of such an approach, and where such an approach can fit in with seeking to understand and monitor the workings of the financial market, a global market with many ramifications.

Chapter 7 summarises the findings of this book and highlights some take-home messages. It highlights the significance and limitations of the work reported and suggests promising future directions.

CHAPTER 2

Background and Literature Survey

T HIS chapter will discuss the research literature on the concept of regime change in the financial market, and on our research topic of the application of Directional Change (DC) to study regime change. In addition, the machine learning techniques that are used in this book are also outlined.

2.1 REGIME CHANGE

Regime Change (RC) is a term more often associated with politics and government rather than with financial markets. In this book, the term is being used to describe what is a significant change in price behaviour in financial markets. The question then arises as to what kind of change in price can be considered as a regime change, rather than simply the normal fluctuations of the financial market. The links between different categories of regime change is noted by [22]: "since the financial crash of 2008, the global financial markets have been subject to prolonged periods in which their behaviour has been dominated by a single, over-arching economic regime, often determined by the stance of monetary policy. When these regimes have changed, the behaviour of the main asset classes (equities, bonds, commodities and currencies) has been drastically affected, and individual asset prices within each class have also had to fit into the overall macro pattern." It is therefore the observed price behaviour in financial markets that can have profound social and political implications.

In the field of macroeconomics, the term regime change is used to explain dramatic breaks in many economic cycles, often with dramatic and unpredictable political, governmental and economic crises causing financial ruptures [31].

Hamilton [32] compared the US unemployment rate since the Second World War and the subsequent periods of economic recession. He discovered that the US economy periodically entered into an episode when the unemployment rate rapidly rose. Such evidence indicated that the economy frequently oscillated between a steady period and a turbulent period, moving from one regime to another. Another example of the fluctuations of market regimes is indicated in the global financial crisis of 2008–2009, where the behaviour of asset prices changed and persisted for many periods. For example, the mean, volatility and correlation patterns in stock returns changed due to the pressures and workings of the financial crisis [8].

Given the evidence of the historical data about the workings of the financial market globally, two types of market regimes are easily recognised and determined: a steady regime with low volatility and economic growth, and a high volatility regime with economic contractions. This leads to the question of how to determine if such regime change has actually occurred.

Ang and Timmermann [8] concluded that shifts from one regime to another may be the result of a major external event, such as the 1973 oil crisis, or the bankruptcy of Lehman Brothers in September 2008. It means that regime change mirrors swings in the economy which may have built up over time, or may be driven by investor expectations [8, 18]. Thus, abrupt changes are considered as a feature of financial data, and there have been a number of studies as to why such sharp changes in fundamentals will show up in asset prices [7, 21, 23, 30, 31, 32].

2.1.1 Regime Change Detection Methods

In order to detect such market changes, researchers monitor the statistical properties of price movements in financial markets. In light of this, some regime detection models are developed to establish such dynamic behaviour.

In 1989, Hamilton [30] proposed a tractable approach to model changes in regimes, which is known as a regime switching model or Markov switching model. It is one of the most popular non-linear time series models to discover hidden patterns in the market. The regime switching model is able to measure multiple breaks and regime changes in the time series structure of financial data. This means the model is capable of characterising the distinctive financial behaviour into different regimes.

The novel feature of the regime switching model is about the switching mechanism of different regimes, where the unobservable states are governed by the first-order Markov chain. The Markov chain assumes that the next state depends only on the current state and not on the sequence of events that precedes it. This mechanism makes the regime switching model suitable to describe the occasional, discrete shifts during different time periods, such as the phenomenon of regime change.

There are several reasons why regime switching models are popular in financial modelling. First, in the view of Ang and Timmermann [8], the idea of regime change is natural and intuitive. It is well documented that economies experience regime changes, some of which are periodic and recurring, such as in recessions and expansions. Others can be the result of unpredictable external political and other events, which affect regime change in fixed income, equities and foreign exchange markets. In the original application regime switching model, Hamilton [30] successfully described cycles of economic activity in the various cycles of recessions and expansions of the financial market.

The second reason is that regime switching models can capture stylized behaviour from financial series data, such as fat tails, ARCH effects, skewness and time-varying correlations [8]. Even when the model is unknown, regime switching models can provide a general approximation for underlying trends. Thus, the regime switching model is capable of capturing such non-linear effects like regime changes. This makes price trends become visible so that the framework of regime changes can be observed. The regime switching model is therefore suitable for explaining distinct patterns during different time periods.

While most researchers have used regime-switching models to establish economic regimes, the significance of these models has always been valued. However, these models are mostly established based on time series analysis. In this book, a new approach is proposed to detect regime change, which is established based on an alternative approach of recording price movements, called Directional Change (DC).

2.2 DIRECTIONAL CHANGE

Financial data contains valuable information that is related to the health of the financial markets. Since both financial theory and its data contain an element of uncertainty, statistical theory and methods of analysis are required in financial data analysis [48].

In the study of financial data, different methods can be applied to analyse a series of data. Many analytical approaches have been used to study and analyse price series under time series analysis. A time series is a series of data points sampled in time order. Under time series, the way to record price series is to sample data points at fixed time intervals. First, we choose a time interval, and then record the data point at the chosen time interval. For example, we can have daily, monthly or annual data. In such cases, time intervals play an important role in time series analysis. For instance, most financial studies involve returns of assets. Therefore, the actual time interval is important in calculating and discussing returns (e.g., daily return, monthly return or annual return) [48].

By contrast, DC is a data driven approach for studying and discovering stylised facts in financial data. It allows us to study financial time series in a data-led and uneven time intervals, which means DC let the data dictate when to sample the data points.

The unique feature of DC is that only the important and significant movements of the market need to be concentrated on. Once a careful defining of the value of the threshold is made, irrelevant details of price evolution are eliminated [5]. As it is the case that financial time series occur at uneven and unpredictably spaced times.

There are several reasons why DC is a suitable approach to study financial data. First, DC is an ideal approach for sampling data at irregular time intervals. For example, the Foreign Exchange market (FX) is open 24 hours a day, 7 days a week [5]. This creates High-Frequency Data (HFD), and the transactions in the FX market vary at different time units of a day. A common way to summarise HFD is to choose a time interval (e.g., hourly, daily or monthly), and then interpolate data points in the time interval. This process runs the risk of losing important information within each time interval.

However, with DC, an event-based approach, researchers are able to handle HFD without losing important information. This is because with DC, the data is sampled at its peaks and trough according to the size of a pre-defined threshold. By choosing different thresholds, researchers are allowed to concentrate on the periods that are considered as important.

Second, the DC approach enables researchers to discover new patterns in the financial market, which cannot be observed by using time series analysis. For example, [27] discovered 12 new scaling laws in foreign exchange markets, which are established based on the DC approach. The new laws extend the catalogue of stylized facts in financial research and enable us to discover new regularities in the financial markets. It proves that DC provides a new angle to explain the market mechanisms, which inspired us to study the mechanisms of regime change in the financial markets with this approach.

2.2.1 The Concept of Directional Change

Guillaume et al. [29] first introduced the concept of DC, as an alternative approach to sample data points. It was used to study stylized facts in FX markets. This concept has also been used by traders, under the name of Zig Zag indicator [43]. Analysts and traders have applied it to remove unnecessary noise in price movements. A formal definition of DC is then provided by [44] (see Appendix A), which is summarised as follows.

Unlike time series, which samples data points at fixed time intervals, DC samples data points at their peaks and troughs in their movement [45]. Under DC, price movements are defined by two types of events: **Directional Change (DC) Event** and **Overshoot (OS) Event**. And with a pre-defined **Threshold**, every price curve can be dissected by these two components.

When summarising price movements using DC, the value of the threshold needs to be pre-defined. The value of the threshold (a percentage) is defined by the observer. It represents how big of a price change the observer considers as significant. Since observers may considers different magnitudes of price change to be significant, they may observe different DC Events and OS Events as data dictates when a DC Event takes place.

A DC Event will be confirmed when the price change reaches the threshold. For example, if the price movement is on an uptrend, a DC Event is confirmed whenever the price drops from the last highest price point (peak). Similarly, if the price movement is on a downtrend, a DC Event is confirmed whenever the price rises from the last lowest price point (trough).

However, a DC Event is not usually immediately followed by an opposite DC Event, but by an OS Event. An OS Event records the price movement from one DC Event to the next. An OS Event is completed while the next DC Event takes place.

Figure 2.1 illustrates the basic concept of DC. Price movements are partitioned into uptrend and downtrend. Uptrend and downtrend correspond to the price in the financial market falling and rising. An uptrend consists of a DC Event and an OS Event (from point A to C). A downtrend is then from point C.

When the price changes from point A to point B, the price change reaches a threshold θ, then a DC Event is confirmed. Point A is then considered as an **Extreme point (EXT)**. And Point B is considered as a **Directional Change Confirmation (DCC) point**. Similarly, the next DC Event is confirmed at point D. The price movement between two DC Events is considered an OS Event (from point B to C).

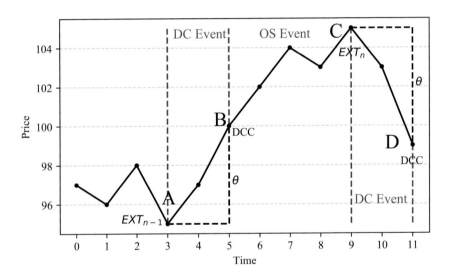

FIGURE 2.1: A hypothetical example of summarising price movements under DC.

Let P_t to be the current price point in the market. A DC Event is calculated as:

$$\left| \frac{P_t - P_{EXT}}{P_{EXT}} \right| \geqslant \theta, \tag{2.1}$$

where P_{EXT} represents the price at extreme point and θ represents the threshold.

2.2.2 Research Using Directional Change

Since the concept of DC was introduced by Guillaume et al. [29], numerous research studies have been conducted under DC. In this section, we review some of the most significant empirical research using DC.

One of the most significant findings in DC is the discovery of new scaling laws. Scaling laws describe the proportional relationship between parameters associated with an object (or system) [24]. It is useful to find regularities in nature. Guillaume et al. [29] first proposed a new scaling law for DC, which is considered as a new quantity to measure volatility, for the description of the price evolution. In contrast with the volatility ratio in time series analysis, it provides an alternative measure of risk.

Later on, another 12 new scaling laws were reported by Glattfelder et al. [27]. More studies on scaling laws and stylized facts in financial markets can be found in the literature (see [4, 5, 37]). The discovery of scaling laws help us to understand stylized facts in the financial market under DC, and enable researchers to discover new regularities which are not observable in time series analysis.

Another research direction under DC is about forecasting. Bakhach et al. [13] focus on the problem of forecasting the price trend's future direction under the DC framework. This study proved that directional changes are predictable and provided an independent variable for forecasting under DC. It lays the foundation for establishing trading strategies based on DC.

The third important research angle is to develop algorithm trading strategies based on DC. Based on stylized facts observed under DC, Golub et al. [28] designed a profitable automated trading model, which is called the Alpha Engine. The authors states this investment strategy not only generates profits, but also provides liquidity to financial markets.

Apart from the Alpha Engine, various studies have been conducted on establishing trading strategies based on DC (see [3, 9, 11, 12, 14]). These studies demonstrate an important point: profitable trading strategies can be developed, and benefit from observing new regularities in financial markets using DC.

As discussed in Guillaume et al. [29], DC provides an alternative way to measure market volatility. Inspired by this, various useful market indicators have been proposed to extract information from financial data. Bisig et al. [17] proposed a probabilistic indicator to quantify market activity, the so-called Scale of Market Quakes (SMQ). This indicator is found useful for detecting crises and regime shifts.

To thoroughly describe price movements and measure the market volatility, Tsang et al. [47] proposed a set of market indicators under DC. The authors argued that these market indicators are useful for profiling markets under DC. In this book, we employed some of the market indicators in Tsang et al. [47], to measure regime changes in financial markets, which are described in the next section.

2.2.3 Directional Change Indicators

There are various ways to measure asset volatility, but for a price series, the volatility is not directly observable [48]. Therefore, statistical methods are needed to measure market evolution.

Tsang et al. [47] introduced a set of indicators under the DC framework. In contrast with the volatility ratio in time series analysis, DC indicators are considered as a complementary way to extract information from data. In this section, we summarise three DC indicators: TMV, T and R, which are then applied to detect regime change in our research.

2.2.3.1 Total Price Movement

This indicator measures the absolute percentage of the price change in a trend. As shown in Figure 2.1, Total Price Movement (TMV) is used to measure the percentage change from point A to point C, normalised by the threshold. It usually measures the total price change of a DC event and an OS event. It is defined as:

$$TMV_{EXT}(n) = \left| \frac{P_{EXT}(n) - P_{EXT}(n-1)}{P_{EXT}(n-1) \times \theta} \right|, \quad (2.2)$$

where $P_{EXT}(n)$ represents the price at nth extreme point, and θ is the threshold defined by researchers.

2.2.3.2 Time for Completion of a Trend

This indicator measures the amount of the physical time (T) that it takes to complete a TMV trend. As shown in Figure 2.1, it measures the time from Time 3 to Time 9. It is defined as:

$$T(n) = t_{EXT}(n) - t_{EXT}(n-1), \qquad (2.3)$$

where $t_{EXT}(n)$ represents the time at nth extreme point.

2.2.3.3 Time–Adjusted Return of DC

This indicator measures the absolute return (R) in a trend. It is calculated by dividing the absolute TMV by the time interval T. It measures the percentage of price change per time unit:

$$R(n) = \frac{TMV_{EXT}(n)}{T(n)} \times \theta, \qquad (2.4)$$

where $R(n)$ represents the value of the time-adjusted return of DC at nth extreme point.

As reported in [45], these three market indicators have the ability to measure market volatility. For example, TMV measures the magnitude of the price change in each change. Higher magnitude indicates a more volatile market. Inspired by this, we employed the DC approach and its indicators to study regime changes in this book. It is worth to note that, the absolute values of TMV and R will be used throughout the book

2.3 MACHINE LEARNING TECHNIQUES

In this section, we will introduce two machine learning techniques: the Hidden Markov Model and the Naïve Bayes classifier. These two machine learning models will be used and combined with DC approach to study regime changes in this book. We use these two techniques because they are both mature, well-established methods. Every method has its assumptions. We have shown that the underlying Hidden Markov Model assumptions are supported by the data that we tested on. Other, more modern, machine methods may give us better results, but we are not at the stage of beauty contest. The research reported in this book is very much a proof of concept, to open up new avenues in regime change detection.

2.3.1 Hidden Markov Model

In the previous section, we discussed how to extract statistical properties through the DC approach. Here, we focus on how to apply Hidden

Markov Models (HMMs) to detect regime change through these statistical properties.

The theory of the HMM was first introduced in the 1960s and 1970s [15]. It was then widely applied in various areas, such as engineering, speech recognition, computational biology and physical sciences. In its applications to the economy, two sequences are considered to exist in the market: the underlying market regime sequence, which remains hidden, and the price sequence, which is observable for all participants. The aim of the HMM is to infer the hidden sequence of market regime by analysing the observed price sequence.

Hamilton[30] adapted the HMM to model changes in financial regimes. He drew the probabilistic inference about whether and when the market regime may have occurred, based on the visible behaviour of the data. By applying the model to the data of the post-war US real Gross National Product (GNP), he suggested that there was a periodic shift from a positive growth rate, to a negative growth rate in the US business cycle. As a result, he indicated that the market fell into recession in 1957–58 and 1979–80, due to the oil price increase in 1957 and the Iranian revolution in 1979.

Related work on the HMM was done by Ghysels [25]. He used the HMM to test whether an economic recovery is equally likely to occur in any particular month of the year. With the HMM, the probability of observing a sequence can be computed. He used the data for business cycles in his work. The result shows that the market has unequal probabilities to switch from recession to expansion, and the economic recovery has a higher chance to occur in the spring and the month of December. Thus, a usually unobservable seasonal pattern is found in business cycle durations by using the HMM, which is quite different from the result of the common linear time series models.

The HMM also can be used in asset allocation. For example, Kritzman et al. [34] showed a way to apply the HMM to forecast market regimes. Their approach is different from other studies as they did not directly model regimes in asset return. Instead, they built the model for a set of economic regime variables: market turbulence, inflation and economic growth. Moreover, they built a set of regime dependent investment strategies, and backtested their performance in the out of sample period. Evidence shows that by using different strategies on the basis of disparate regimes, investment performances are significantly improved.

In our view, the central new feature of our work is the combination of using the observed variables under DC, together with the HMM. Given the oscillation of the financial market between expansion and contraction, and the regime changes that brings it with it, the HMM is a well-suited model for gaining insight into those changes of market regime.

2.3.1.1 Definition of HMM

An HMM is a statistical model which enable us to relate a sequence of observations to a sequence of hidden states [40]. In an HMM, we assume that there are two types of sequences: a sequence of observations and a sequence of hidden states. The observation sequence is visible to the observer, but the state sequence is not directly observable; in other words, it is hidden from the observer.

The HMM is based on the assumption of the Markov chain [33]. A Markov chain is a stochastic model which describes a sequence of events in which the probability that one event only depends on its previous event. The Markov assumption can be described as:

$$P(q_i = a | q_1 ... q_{i-1}) = P(q_i = a | q_{i-1}) \qquad (2.5)$$

The HMM assumes that the state sequence follows a first-order Markov chain. That means the probability of a particular state depends only on the previous state. In summary, an HMM is a statistical model that allows us to consider both the observed data and the hidden states. In many cases, the events that we are interested in are hidden: we don't observe them directly. The HMM allows us to discover the hidden states, given the sequence of observations.

2.3.1.2 Parameters of HMM

The general structure of an HMM is described in Figure 2.2. The model is described by three parameters. The first one is the transition probability matrix A, where $A = a_{ij} ... a_{NN}$, each a_{ij} represents the probability of moving from state i to state j. Since the HMM assumes that the transition between any two states follows a Markov chain, the probability of one state depends solely on the previous state.

The second parameter is a sequence of observation likelihoods B, where $B = b_i(O_t)$. It is also called the emission probabilities, which represents the probability of an observation O_t being generated from a state i.

And the last parameter is the initial probability distribution π_i, which is the probability that the Markov chain will start in first state i [33].

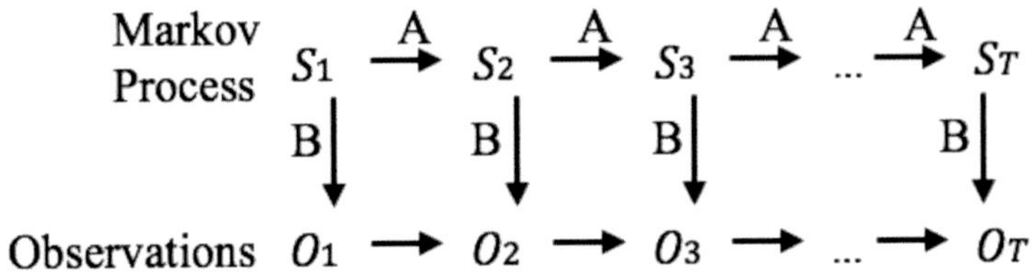

$$\begin{array}{c} \text{Markov} \\ \text{Process} \end{array} \quad S_1 \xrightarrow{A} S_2 \xrightarrow{A} S_3 \xrightarrow{A} \dots \xrightarrow{A} S_T$$

with each B arrow pointing down to:

$$\text{Observations} \quad O_1 \rightarrow O_2 \rightarrow O_3 \rightarrow \dots \rightarrow O_T$$

FIGURE 2.2: A general structure of a Hidden Markov Model.

Given a sequence of observation O, the purpose of using a HMM is to find the "hidden" sequence S. To do that, we need to learn the parameters of an HMM, that is the transition probability matrix A and the emission probabilities B. The input to the learning algorithm would be an unlabelled sequence of observations O and the number of potential hidden states S. For example, in this book, two hidden states are considered to have occurred in the financial market. Thus, the state variable could either be S_1 or S_2.

From the observed data, we want to learn the sequence of hidden states as well as the emission probabilities. We want to find a sequence of hidden states and the emission probabilities that maximally fits the observed data.

For this purpose, we apply an HMM package called depmixS4, which implements the HMM in R programming language [51]. It applies the iterative Expectation-Maximization (EM) algorithm by default, to learn both the transition probabilities and the emission probabilities of the HMM from the input data.

2.3.1.3 Expectation-Maximization Algorithm

The standard algorithm for HMM learning parameters is the forward-backward, or Baum–Welch algorithm. It is a special case of the Expectation-Maximization algorithm (or EM for short) [33].

The algorithm lets us learn both the transition probabilities matrix A and the emission probabilities matrix B of the HMM. It is an iterative algorithm. At first, it computes an initial estimate for the probabilities, then using those estimates to compute a better estimate, and so on, iteratively improving the probabilities that it learns, until it finds both the transition probabilities and the emission probabilities that best fits the input data [33].

Before implementing the algorithm, we need to make an assumption that the observation sequence is governed by two Gaussian distributions. This is because, in this book, we assume that the hidden state sequence consists of two types of regimes, the state variable could only be S_1 or S_2. And the observation sequence is continuous data, which is assumed to follow Gaussian distributions. Therefore, the observation sequence can be represented by two Gaussian distributions.

Given a sequence of unlabelled observations, the task of the EM algorithm is to, first, estimate which state the individual observation belongs to, and second, estimate the parameters of the two Gaussian distributions. There are also parameters of the HMM, where the transition probabilities A are the likelihoods of state change, and the emission probabilities B are the two Gaussian distributions.

The EM algorithm iteration performs between two steps: the expectation step or E step, and the maximization step or M step. First, the algorithm will start with an initial estimate of the parameters of HMM $\lambda = (A, B)$. Then, in the E step, given each input data, the expect value of the emission probability and transition probability are computed. In the M step, those computed probabilities are then used to re-estimate the new HMM parameters A, B. Then the algorithm will repeatedly carry out these two steps until convergence.

2.3.2 Naïve Bayes Classifier

Our other innovation, which is explored in Chapter 5 in this book, is to track the on-going regime changes in the markets. In particular, we want to track the market to see whether the market is entering into an abnormally volatile regime, using both the information of historical regime changes and the financial data that is observed up to present. This is because we consider the regime changes in the past can provide some useful information about the regime changes at present.

The Naïve Bayes' Classifier (NBC) offers the ability to solve this kind of problem. The model is established based on applying the Bayes' theorem, which is named after Reverend Thomas Bayes, who first provided an equation that allows new evidence to update beliefs [16]. The NBC allows us to describe the probability of an event, based on the prior knowledge of status that might be related to this event. In our case, the model enables us to calculate the probability of the market being in a particular regime, based on the information of previous regime changes.

The NBC is a statistical algorithm for the classification task. It simplifies the computation involved by assuming all features are independent given class. This assumption is called Class Conditional Independence, and this is why the model is considered "naive" [35]. Although this is a strong assumption, in practice, the NBC often performs better than more sophisticated classifiers [41].

2.3.2.1 Definition of Naïve Bayes Classifier

The Naïve Bayes' classifier is a statistical classification model which is established based on Bayes' theorem. The mathematical form of Bayes' theorem is described as:

$$p(A|B) = \frac{p(B|A)p(A)}{p(B)} \tag{2.6}$$

where A and B represent two events. $p(A|B)$ represents the conditional probability of event A given that event B has occurred. Similarly, $p(B|A)$ represents the conditional probability of event B given that event A has occurred. $p(A)$ and $p(B)$ represent the probability of observing events A and B, respectively.

With the application of the Bayes' theorem, the classifier allows us to calculate the likelihood that an event will occur, based on the prior knowledge of conditions that might be related to the event. In this book, it allows us to calculate the likelihood of the occurrence of a market regime, based on the information of previous regime changes. Using the Bayes' theorem, the NBC is constructed as follows:

$$p(C_i|x) = \frac{p(C_i)p(x|C_i)}{p(x)} \tag{2.7}$$

where $p(C_i|x)$ is the probability a particular class C_i has occurred given that the observed variable x is seen. $p(x|C_i)$ is the conditional probability that an event belonging to C_i has associated observation variables x. $p(C_i)$ is called the prior probability that an event C_i has occurred, regardless of the x value. $p(x)$ is the marginal probability that the observation variable x is seen [6].

Classification using the NBC includes two phases, the training phase and the testing phase. In the training phase, the model is trained to a given data set. And in the testing phase, the model is used to classify data with an unknown label. For example, suppose we have a training set of samples x, and the class label of each sample is denoted by C. The model works in the following steps: (i) calculate the prior probability for the given class label $p(C)$, (ii) calculate the condition probability of each sample for each class $p(x|C)$, and (iii) combine these values using the Bayes' theorem to calculate the posterior probability $p(C|x)$.

CHAPTER 3

Regime Change Detection Using Directional Change Indicators

A Regime change is a significant change in the collective trading behaviour in a financial market. Being able to detect the occurrence of regime change could lead to a better understanding and monitoring of financial markets. In this chapter, a novel method is proposed to detect regime change, which makes use of a data-driven approach, that of Directional Change (DC).

Compared to the conventional approach of using time series analysis, DC is an alternative approach to sample price movement. As variables observed under time series do not apply to DC, our first contribution is the identification of a new relevant indicator for regime change detection. Our second contribution is the comparison of both the DC approach and time series analysis, and their ability to achieve regime change detection. The ability of both approaches in regime change detection is examined over a period of market uncertainty, that of Brexit, in June, 2016. The results demonstrated that the DC approach is as effective as the time series approach in detecting regime changes. Moreover, the DC approach is encouraging because some market regime changes are detected under DC, that are not found under time series. That means they support each other in the detection of regime changes, and can also provide extra information to complement each other. Together, regime changes detected under both DC and time series provide a better insight into the market, which market participants and regulators could benefit from.

This chapter is organised as follows: Section 3.1 introduces our motivation to study regime changes based on the approach of Directional Change. Section 3.2 describes our designed approach to recognise regime changes. The process of the experiment is presented in Section 3.3. The results of the experiment are discussed in Section 3.4. Section 3.5 concludes this chapter.

3.1 INTRODUCTION

The booms and crashes in financial markets have profound social and political implications. Such changes are often associated with events like a financial crisis or abrupt changes in government policy [31]. In order to detect such significant changes, researchers monitor the statistical properties of price movements in financial markets. For example, the mean, volatility and correlation patterns in stock returns are found to be different at the beginning, middle, and the end of the global financial crisis of 2008–2009 [8]. And when such statistical properties change significantly, researchers say that the market has gone through a regime change [8, 31, 34].

In this book, regime change is considered to occur as a result of changes in trading behaviour among the traders. Unfortunately, in reality, one can never directly observe the changes in trading behaviour. Alternatively, one can only observe price changes in a market. One could attempt to observe a change of traders' behaviour indirectly by observing the price movements in a market. If a change in the statistical properties of the price movement is observed, then it is possible to conclude that a regime change has taken place. This is the approach taken by most researchers.

Regime change is usually measured under the framework of time series [39]. Hamilton concluded that time series can show the dramatic breaks in market behaviour during economic downturns. He proposed a regime switching model to measure such abrupt changes in economic variables [31].

Regime switching models are time-series models, in which parameters are allowed to take on different values in a number of regimes [39].

These models usually measure regime changes based on the statistical properties that were observed under time series.

Ang and Timmermann [8] applied the regime switching model to equity returns, interest rates, and foreign exchange returns, and discussed how regime changes are modelled. They concluded that regime changes could be a result of a change in economic policy or a major financial event, such as the bankruptcy of the US investment bank Lehman Brothers in 2008. Another suggestion is that changing market regimes could also be driven by investor expectations.

Regime change presents significant challenges to investors: the performance of their trading strategies generally depends on the market continuing to behave as before. This assumption is especially important for trading algorithms that rely on machine learning. When the collective trading behaviour changes in the market, trading strategies may need to change. Therefore, those who are able to recognise when there is a regime change would have an edge over those who cannot. Kritzman et al. [34] demonstrated how to apply regime switching models to forecast regime changes in the market. They found that regime-based asset allocation could help investors avoid large losses and deliver significant benefits. Being able to recognise regime changes could also help regulators to monitor the market and react when necessary to maintain its stability. Thus, being able to detect regime change is useful for both traders and regulators.

Since most of the studies of regime change are based on the framework of time series, in this book, a data-driven approach is chosen to recognise regime change in the financial market, that of Directional Change (or DC for short). This approach differs from the conventional studies in that it does not rely on the statistical properties found in time series. By contrast, it measures the statistical properties that are observed under different price events, which are defined under the framework of DC [29]. Details of DC were introduced in Section 2.2.

DC is an alternative approach to the recording of price movements. The pioneering works on this have shown that DC provides a way to extract information from data [47]. Also, the indicators that are developed under the framework of DC allow us to observe features that may not be recognised in time series [47]. Encouraged by that finding, the DC approach and one of the DC indicators are chosen in this research chapter to detect regime change.

The proposed approach includes two parts: first, the statistical properties of the price movements are observed through the DC approach and summarised by one of the DC indicators, namely DC Return (or R for short). Second, different market regimes are discovered from the DC indicator through the Hidden Markov Model (HMM). The model is used to learn "hidden states" from the input data. Thus, the data from the same state belongs to one regime, and the change between states is considered as regime change.

Detecting regime change under the DC approach is replicating what is done in time series: observing the statistical properties taking place in price movements. The only difference is that the statistical properties are observed under DC. Since the method using DC is a departure from the usual way for the study of regime change, some questions may be raised: By observing statistical properties defined under DC, could we detect regime change? Would regime change detected under DC be the same as regime change detected under time series? Or would they be different? And how can people benefit from the study of regime change?

To answer these questions, the DC approach and the time series approach were both used for testing whether regime changes occurred during the period of Brexit, or the UK's referendum over continuing membership of the EU on 23 June 2016. Results were announced on 24 June, with the "remain" side expected to win. But after the exit campaign won, David Cameron, the Prime Minister then resigned. Theresa May was later elected by the Conservative Party to become the new Prime Minister.

Such political upheavals caused the British pound to plunge to a 30-year low on the day the UK voted to leave the European Union, and there were big sell-offs in the global stock market [38]. How did the financial market react to these political changes? Did it go through regime changes? If so, when did the market enter a new regime? Did the market return to the original regime afterwards? In an attempt to answer these questions, we looked at the data from the Foreign Exchange Market from May to July 2016. We wanted to see what the data told us about this dramatic period of upheavals.

This study presents an approach under the DC framework for detecting regime changes. Under the DC approach, the DC indicator was not only able to detect regime change during the Brexit period, which was also detectable under time series, it was also able to pick up regime changes in the market, which was not detectable by the time series indicator. We therefore argue that we have added a useful tool for regime change detection.

3.2 METHODOLOGY

In this section, we proposed an approach to detect regime changes under the DC framework. This approach is contrasted to the conventional time series approach. We emphasise that this is not a comparison for which is the better approach, DC or time series. The aim is to find out whether the two approaches together would enable us to pick up more useful signals from the data; in other words, whether one could gain by looking at the data from two sources.

Figure 3.1 shows the procedure of our methodology. Both DC and time series would start with the same data. Under the DC framework, data is summarised as DC events (uptrends and downtrends). Then we measure the R of each trend. These R values are fed into the Hidden Markov Model (HMM) for regime change detection. And under the time series framework, a 5-minute series is extracted from the data. Returns for each of these 5-minute periods are then computed. Based on these returns, the daily volatility is computed. These volatility values are fed into the HMM for regime detection. In the following, we shall elaborate each of these processes.

Under DC, the price movement is summarised under a pre-defined threshold. Glattfelder et al. [27] point out that the power law is exhibited in DC observations. This suggests that, by and large, the same stylised facts can be observed under different thresholds. Therefore, throughout this chapter, the threshold value is arbitrarily set as: $\theta = 0.4\%$.

Then, the DC indicator and the time series indicator will be fed into the HMM with the same set up:

1. DC indicator: R

2. time series indicator: *realised volatility RV*

The aim of the experiment is to detect regime change from the corresponding indicators in both DC and time series using HMM. While implementing the HMM, the number of states and the sequence of observation data needs to be decided. Since the observation data in this chapter is continuous rather than discrete, we use the Gaussian distribution for the model density. Here, an HMM with two states is used. It means that only two regimes are assumed to have occurred in the market: Regime 1 or Regime 2. This is justified by the fact that we only cover a relatively short period of time (two months).

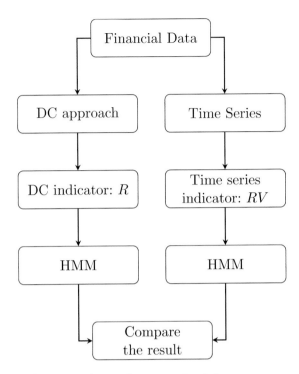

FIGURE 3.1: The procedure of our methodology.

3.2.1 DC Indicator

Under the DC approach, the DC indicator R is used as the observation data in the HMM. The chosen DC indicator was found by trial and error. It measures the return for each price trend. It not only measures the total price movements of each trend (**Total Price Movement**, denoted by **TMV**), but also measures the **Time** it takes to complete the trend (denoted by **T**). It reflects both the magnitude and the time duration of price movements, which are orthogonal measures of volatility under DC. The input and output of the model are as follows:

1. Input: the absolute values of the DC indicator R for each DC trend, where trends are generated using second-to-second data with a threshold $\theta = 0.4\%$.

2. Output: the state symbol of each input data (either Regime 1 or Regime 2).

In this experiment, the DC indicator R is log-transformed as follows:

$$LR[t] := log(R[t]), \qquad (3.1)$$

where L represents the log transformation of the DC indicator and $R[t]$ represents the value of R at time t.

3.2.2 Time Series Indicator

For the time series approach, the realised volatility RV of the data is used as the input of the HMM. Realised volatility is one of the common time series tools to measure volatility from high-frequency financial data [48]. The mechanism of realised volatility is simple: the daily realised volatility is simply calculated by summing up intra-day squared returns. In this chapter, we are calculating the daily realised volatility based on the 5-minute log return.

Suppose r_t is the 5-minute log return of an asset at time t. Then the realised volatility RV can be defined as:

$$RV(t) = \sum_{i=1}^{n} r_t^2(i), \qquad (3.2)$$

where n is the number of 5-minute log return in one trading day. The input and output of the model are as follows:

1. Input: realised daily volatility RV computed by 5-minute returns within the day.

2. Output: the state symbol of each input data.

Finally, the regimes that are detected by the DC indicator are compared with the regimes that are detected by the time series indicator.

It is worth noting that, since volatility can only be computed by a series of returns, we use daily volatility (computed from 5-minute returns) in time series. Under the DC framework, we input to HMM the R per trend. Since we used second-by-second data to compute DCs, we could theoretically detect regime changes by their seconds. The same is not possible in time series. Even if we use second-by-second returns to compute returns, we can only compute volatility over a period of time (say per minute).

3.3 EXPERIMENTS

3.3.1 Data Sets

A second-by-second database is used in this experiment, which composed of three currency pairs: EUR-GBP, GBP-USD and EUR-USD[1]. The data spanned two months, from 23 May, 2016 to 22 July, 2016, which covered the UK's EU referendum, which took place on 23 June, 2016. We wanted to see if regime changes took place following the unexpected result of the referendum. For the DC approach, the DC indicator was calculated based on the second-by-second observed closing price. For the time series approach, the indicator was calculated based on the 5-minute log return.

3.3.2 Hidden Markov Model

In order to detect regime change from our input data, we made use of the Dependent Mixture Models package in R (depmixS4) [51]. The process was organised as follows:

1. Fitting a Hidden Markov Model to our input data (see Section 3.2).

2. Determining the posterior probability of being in one of two market regimes (Regime 1 or Regime 2).

3. Determining the state symbol (Regime 1 or Regime 2) of each input data.

3.4 EMPIRICAL RESULTS

In this section, we present the results of regime changes that are detected under both DC and time series. It is clear that choosing the number of regimes is a challenging problem of regime detection. Here, we decide to detect two types of regimes from our data sets. Thus, a two-state Hidden Markov Model is used. The data will be classified into two regimes: Regime 1 and Regime 2. Under DC, the trends in

---

[1]The data which was used in this chapter is provided by the Centre for Computational Finance and Economic Agents (CCFEA), University of Essex. It was purchased from Kibot, a data vendor. This contains tick-to-tick data.

Regime 2 carry higher DC returns R (as illustrated in Figure 3.2a). Under time series, higher volatility is exhibited in the market in Regime 2 (see Figure 3.2b).

3.4.1 EUR–GBP

Figure 3.2 depicts the detected regime changes of EUR-GBP. Details of the regimes are shown in Table 3.1. Price movements are classified into two regimes: Regime 1 and Regime 2. These regimes are detected using DC indicator and time series indicator individually.

Under the use of the DC indicator, two regimes are established (see Figure 3.2a). Figure 3.2a shows that HMM classified the market to be in Regime 2 when the return R is high, Regime 1 when the return is low. Regime 2 starts from 23 June to 24 June, which covered the period of the UK's EU referendum. Thus, this regime might have been triggered by the UK's EU referendum, which took place on 23 June 2016.

A second regime change was picked up on 14 July 2016. But that only lasted within a day. This regime is considered to have been triggered by the following events:

1. The Bank of England (BoE) decided to hold its benchmark rate at 0.5% on 14 July 14 2016 (see [1]).

2. Theresa May became the new British Prime Minister on 13 July 2016.

The BoE's decision was announced on 14 July 2106, after its meeting ending on 13 July 2016. Even though expectations had risen that the bank would take action to mitigate the negative impact of Brexit, the bank still surprised the financial markets by holding its benchmark rate [26]. Sterling responded to the decision by gaining 2.7 per cent against the dollar on the session [26]. As a result, our indicator DC return R measured a significant jump on 14 July and then indicated the regime change of the market from Regime 1 into Regime 2 (see Figure 3.2a).

Furthermore, the second regime change might also have responded to a major political event. That of Theresa May taking over as the next Prime Minister of the UK on 13 July 2016, and our indicator measured a regime change on the morning of 14 July [42].

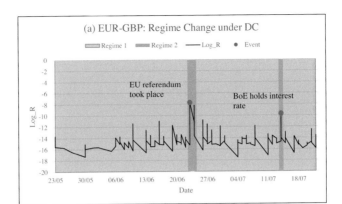

(a)

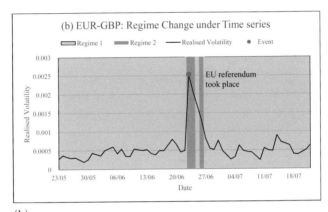

(b)

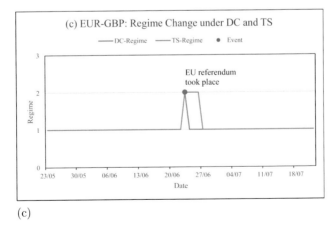

(c)

FIGURE 3.2: Regime changes in EUR–GBP. (a) Regime changes under DC. (b) Regime changes under time series (TS). (c) The comparison of regime changes under both approaches.

With the use of time series indicator, the periods with large volatility are classified as Regime 2, and periods with low volatility are classified as Regime 1 (see Figure 3.2b). The HMM identified a regime change from 23 June to 26 June. The gap shown in Figure 3.2b was due to the fact that there was no trading on 25 June. Significant changes in the daily returns emerged the day of and the day after the referendum results were announced.

Figure 3.2c contrasts the results between DC and time series. The intra-day regime change picked up by DC was not shown in Figure 3.2c because we used days as units there (volatility was computed in days in time series, as explained above). Viewing the data from different angles, DC and time series were able to spot different regime classifications in the market. This was to be expected. They both picked up a regime change in the market, starting on 23 June 2016, when the UK referendum was underway. This is encouraging because their results support each other. The differences in the boundary of regime change could help traders to judge from two different perspectives, which would be useful.

Table 3.1: Time periods of regimes in EUR-GBP.

Directional Change: R	
Number	Regime 1
1	23/05/2016 04:50:46–23/06/2016 16:46:42
2	24/06/2016 12:15:31–14/07/2016 07:00:21
3	14/07/2016 09:44:16–22/07/2016 07:12:26
Time Series: RV	
1	23/05/2016–22/06/2016
2	27/06/2016–22/07/2016

Directional Change: R	
Number	Regime 2
1	23/06/2016 17:01:59–24/06/2016 11:15:07
2	14/07/2016 07:03:12–14/07/2016 07:05:01
Time Series: RV	
1	23/06/2016–26/06/2016

3.4.2 GBP–USD

Figure 3.3 showed the resulting regime changes of GBP-USD under both DC and time series. Details of the regimes are shown in Table B.2

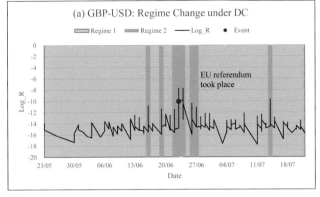

(a)

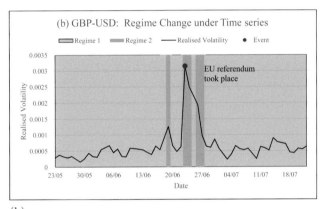

(b)

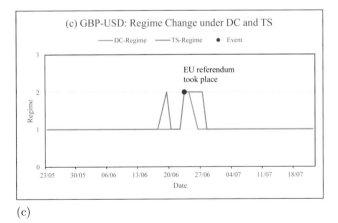

(c)

FIGURE 3.3: Regime change in GBP–USD. (a) Regime changes under DC. (b) Regime changes under time series (TS). (c) The comparison of regime changes under both approaches.

in the Appendix B. The data is also classified into two regimes. These regimes might have been triggered by the following political and financial events:

1. The Gilt yields fell to a record low on 13 June 2016 [36].

2. The implied sterling volatility surged toward its record high since the financial crisis in October 2008 [36].

3. UK's EU referendum took place on 23 June 2016.

With the use of the DC indicator, a few periods of Regime 2 emerged from 16 June to 14 July (see Figure 3.3a, which does not show intra-day regime changes because we use days as units there). Under time series indicator, two periods of Regime 2 were found (see Figure 3.3b, where the gap on 26 June was due to no trading on that day).

The periods of Regime 2 found under DC and TS are contrasted in Figure 3.3c. The results are similar to those in EUR-GBP. Both DC and time series picked up regime changes which started on 23 June, the day when the UK voted for Brexit.

DC picked up a few intra-day regime changes, one of which overlapped the first regime change under time series on 19 June. Regime changes found under DC and time series overlapped in major periods. There is a sufficient difference to allow both approaches to co-exist to provide viewers with twin perspectives.

3.4.3 EUR–USD

Figure 3.4 shows regime change detected in EUR-USD. Details of the regimes are shown in Table B.1 in the Appendix B. DC picked up one continuous period of Regime 1 from 23 June to 24 June 2016 (see Figure 3.4a). A few more regime changes were picked up in this data set under time series (see Figure 3.4b). Having said that, they both picked up regime changes when the UK made its vote for Brexit. The difference between DC and time series could help to enrich the viewers' insight into the market.

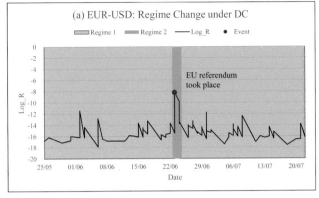

(a)

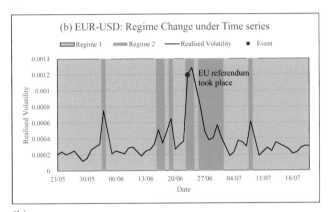

(b)

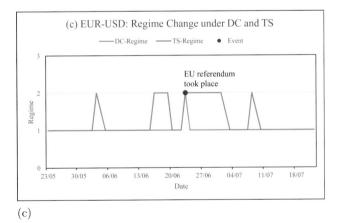

(c)

FIGURE 3.4: Regime change in EUR–USD. (a) Regime changes under DC. (b) Regime changes under time series (TS). (c) The comparison of regime changes under both approaches.

3.4.4 Distribution of the Indicator R

Apart from the general picture of the detected regime changes, there is also a need to know how the DC indicator R would distribute in terms of different regimes. Figure 3.5 shows the distribution of the DC indicator: R. For each data set, the indicator is classified in terms of two market regimes. This shows that the market regimes are not simply separated by the value of the indicator, but are classified according to their distribution in the data set.

3.4.5 Discussion

This experiment shows how regime change detection could provide a better insight into the financial market.

First, meaningful market regimes are able to be found by using both the DC approach and the time series approach. The foreign exchange market is proved to respond to a major political event, in this case, the Brexit referendum. Results show that under both approaches, regime changes are detected on 23 June 2016, the day of the Brexit vote (see Figures 3.2, 3.3 and 3.4). These regime changes illustrate how the foreign exchange markets are influenced by an unexpected political event in terms of regime change.

Secondly, the DC approach complements the time series approach in regime change detection. As they both start with the same data, regime changes observed in DC and time series should not be completely different. Results show that they overlap, especially over the Brexit announcement period. For example, using the DC approach, a second market regime (Regime 2) is recognised from the data of EUR-GBP, which runs from 23 June to 24 June. Correspondingly, under time series, a Regime 2 is also recognised and sustained over the period from 23 June to 26 June. These two market regimes are detected under different frameworks, but they both responded to the same political event, that of the Brexit vote, and its announced result. This is encouraging, because it suggests that the variables that we picked (volatility in time series, and R in DC) are relevant, and they picked up meaningful signals, for identification.

However, the regime changes detected under these two frameworks are not identical. As DC and time series sample data differently, they should pick up different signals, and therefore produce different results. For instance, one extra regime change is detected under DC, which is

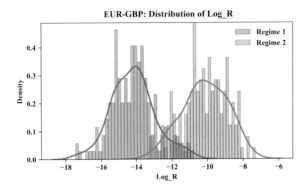

(a)

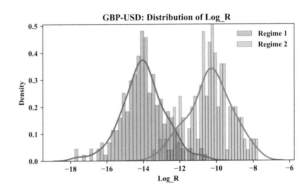

(b)

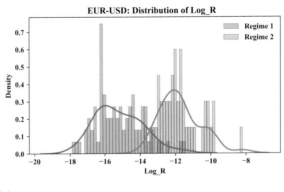

(c)

FIGURE 3.5: (a) Distribution of the indicator R in EUR–GBP. (b) Distribution of the indicator R in GBP–USD. (c) Distribution of the indicator R in EUR–USD.

not registered under time series (see Table 3.1, the column of Regime 2). This is also encouraging, because the two systems provide information to complement each other.

Thirdly, this experiment suggests that regime changes can be registered using different criteria. Under the time series approach, regime changes are measured using the daily volatility. And under the DC approach, the DC return is used to measure the price movements. As both the time series and DC indicator both picked up meaningful signals of regime change, these two chosen indicators are proved to be useful in regime change detection. Results show that the price movements did change in both volatility and in DC return. And together they both confirmed that trading behaviour in the market did change significantly in response to political and financial events.

In practice, market participants and regulators may apply time series and DC independently for regime change detection, which would enhance their understanding of the market. Better detection of regime changes helps better monitoring of financial markets. The next stage of our research is to detect regime changes soon after it happens, which will contribute to building financial early warning systems.

3.5 CONCLUSION

This chapter presents an approach to detect regime change in the financial market. This is the first attempt to detect regime changes under the DC framework, which is different from the conventional time series approach. It is also the first time a DC indicator was used in a Hidden Markov Model.

As variables observed under time series do not apply to DC, our first challenge was to identify relevant DC indicators for regime change detection. We have demonstrated that by using the DC return indicator R, regime change can be detected through the Hidden Markov Model. We argue that this is a significant breakthrough.

In our experiments, the DC approach (using the DC return indicator) is compared to a time series approach (using the volatility indicator) in regime change detection. Results demonstrated that the two approaches pick up regime change periods that are similar, but not identical to each other, in June 2016 over the period of the Brexit referendum. To understand the results, one must realise that R is a different way to measure volatility: the bigger the R value suggests a bigger price change in a shorter period of time. Under time series, we measure volatility by the variance of returns. By using both DC and time series, one can pick up similar, but not identical signals from the market. Used together, DC and time series give us a better understanding of what happened in the market over this period.

Both the DC and time series approaches picked up regime changes on the day before the Brexit referendum result was announced on 24 June 2016. Both indicators suggest that traders reacted ahead of the results. The volatile regime detected under time series lasted for three days; whereas, the volatile regime detected by DC lasted for less than one day. This is because they determine regime changes by different criteria (variance of returns in time series, R in DC).

In our experiment, the DC approach picked up regime changes which were not registered under that of time series. For example, a second volatile regime (Regime 2) is identified in the EUR-GBP data under DC, which was not detected under time series (see Figure 3.2). This change of regime coincided with the news of Theresa May becoming the British Prime Minister. In other words, during the Brexit period, the DC approach did not only pick up signals that support the time series approach, but also it detected signals which were not measured under time series. Our analysis above serves as a proof of the concept of regime change detection under the DC framework. We do not claim to provide a comprehensive analysis of the foreign exchange market during the Brexit period; doing so goes beyond the scope of this chapter.

To summarise, we have presented the first attempt to detect regime changes under DC. We have identified an effective indicator (namely R) for regime change detection. We have confirmed that the DC approach complements that of the time series approach in regime change detection. Together, they allow us to better understand the volatility changes in the market. The regime changes found coincided with major political and financial events. Being able to recognise regime change in the financial market allows us to have a better insight into the market. Such insight could support future research in helping traders establish trading strategies under different market regimes, and regulators to monitor volatility of the market.

CHAPTER 4

Classification of Normal and Abnormal Regimes in Financial Markets

W HEN financial market conditions change, traders adopt different strategies. The traders' collective behaviour may cause significant changes in the statistical properties of price movements. When this happens, the market is said to have gone through "regime changes". The purpose of this chapter is to characterise what is a "normal market regime" as well as what is an "abnormal market regime", under observations in Directional Change (DC).

Our study starts with historical data from 10 financial markets. For each market, we focus on a period of time in which significant events could have triggered regime changes. The observations of regime changes in these markets are then positioned in a designed two-dimensional indicator space based on DC.

Our results suggest that the normal regimes from different markets share similar statistical characteristics. In other words, with our observations, it is possible to distinguish normal regimes from abnormal regimes.

This is significant, because, for the first time, we can tell whether a market is in a normal regime by observing the DC indicators in the market. This opens the door for future work to be able to dynamically monitor the market for regime change.

The remainder of this chapter is organised as follows: Section 4.1 introduces the objective of this chapter. Section 4.2 introduces the methodology for characterising different types of market regimes. Section 4.3 describes our experiments. Section 4.4 presents the results of the experiments and discusses our main findings. Section 4.5 concludes the chapter.

4.1 INTRODUCTION

Prices in financial markets are records of transactions between market participants. When significant political and economic events take place, traders may have to adopt different trading strategies to counteract them. When that happens, their collective behaviour could change significantly – researchers call such changes in the market "regime changes". Regime changes can therefore be seen as a reflection of significant changes in the statistical properties of price movements in the financial markets.

A common approach to detect what is regime change is to analyse the statistical properties of time series [8]. Here, market volatility is calculated over time. When volatility has changed significantly over a period of time, we may conclude that regime changes have taken place.

Thus, DC is an alternative way to that of time series to summarise what are financial price movements [27]. Unlike time series, under this approach the data is not sampled at fixed intervals. A data point is sampled only when the market has changed direction. The market is considered to have changed direction when the price has dropped by a certain percentage (which is called the threshold) from the last market high point, or has risen by the threshold, from the last market low point. In other words, DC and time series are looking at the same data, but from different angles. Therefore, there is no reason why one cannot detect regime change using DC series.

Tsang et al. [47] introduced a number of indicators to measure volatility in DC series. Based on these indicators, we introduced a new method to detect regime changes under DC in our first research chapter, Chapter 3. Basically, this approach was used to collect values of one DC-based indicator in a DC summary, and put this data to a Hidden Markov Model, which classified the input into two regimes. The details of this approach will be summarised in the next section.

Using this approach, we then discovered that there was regime change in the wake of the Pound-to-Dollar (GBP–USD) exchange market after the British public voted for Brexit, in June 2016. The market became significantly more volatile following the time the result of the referendum was announced. For convenience, we label the regime with greater volatility as an "abnormal regime", as opposed to the "normal regime" in which the market operated for most of the time.

The aim of this chapter is to investigate whether normal regimes in different markets at different times share similar statistical properties. Being able to characterise normal regimes is useful. This is because it would enable us to generalise as to what are the results across different markets and times. It moves us one step closer to being able to monitor the financial market to locate what is its regime position while trading (this topic will be left for future research). For example, if the market is moving away from the normal regime, a trader may consider closing their position or adopting a different trading strategy.

4.2 METHODOLOGY

In this section, a new method is proposed to recognise what are the different types of market regimes in the financial market. Firstly, financial data is sampled by a data-driven approach, which resulted in a series of DCs [27]. Values of a certain indicator are observed from the DC series [47]. With values in this DC-indicator, the Hidden Markov Model (HMM), a machine learning model, is employed to detect regime changes [46]. Finally, new research in this chapter, is that the periods of market regimes are profiled in a two-dimensional DC-indicator space. By observing the market regimes in the indicator space, we attempted to locate the relative positions of normal regimes and abnormal regimes.

4.2.1 Summarising Financial Data in DC

Simply put, traders buy and sell for profit in financial markets. And then the transaction prices are recorded, which forms the basis of financial data. Transactions also take place in irregular time, there may be many transactions in one second, but none in the next. Thus, raw transaction data is therefore difficult to clearly be able to reason from, because of its irregularity. Most researchers would summarise the data using time series, where one data point is recorded at the end of each fixed time interval. For example, the final price on each trading day can be recorded as the "daily closing price". Time series analysis is commonly used to summarise financial data in this way.

This chapter adopts an alternative way to summarise financial data. It is based on the concept of DC [27]. When summarising data under DC, it is the observer who determines what constitutes a significant change in the data. This significant percentage of change is called the "threshold". Whenever the price changes in the opposite direction of the current trend and reaches the threshold, the extreme price is retrospectively recorded as a data point. Thus, financial data is recorded as a series of trends, defined by the extreme points (i.e., the peak and trough). Details of DC can be found in [47]. By recording data in this way, the use of DC ensures that the significant changes in the market are captured, whenever they occurred.

Figure 4.1 shows an example of summarising financial data under DC. When prices change from A to B, if the change is greater than or equal to the threshold, then AB is called a "Directional Change Event" (DC Event for short). Point "A" is retrospectively recognised as an extreme point, which ended the previous downtrend and started the current uptrend. From Point "C", the price drops by the specified threshold. Therefore, C ended the current uptrend and started the next downtrend. The price movement from Point "B" to Point "C" is called an "Overshoot Event" (OS Event for short). In other words, a trend (e.g., from "A" to "C" in Figure 4.1) comprised a DC Event and an OS Event. The market is thus partitioned into a series of alternating uptrends and downtrends, which could be read as the bull and bear markets that traders are familiar with.

Therefore, to help with the analysis of DC series, [47] proposed a number of indicators. Below, we introduce indicators used in this chapter. The percentage price change in a trend measured by an indicator is called "Total Price Movement" (**TMV** for short). To allow us to compare DC series generated by different thresholds, we normalised the price changes by the threshold θ:

$$TMV = \frac{|Ps - Pe|/Ps}{\theta} \tag{4.1}$$

where Ps is the price at the start of the trend, and Pe is the price at the end of the trend.

The time that it takes to complete a trend is measured by another indicator which is called "Time" (**T** for short). "Return" (**R** for short) takes the usual meaning, which measures price change over time:

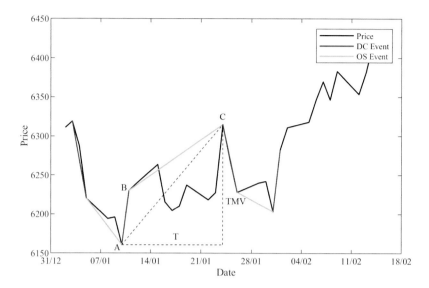

FIGURE 4.1: An example data summary under DC. The black curve describes the daily price of the FTSE 100 Index (32 trading days from 2 January 2007 to 14 February 2007). The red lines describe the DC events and the green lines describe the OS events.

$$R = \frac{|TMV| \times \theta}{T} \qquad (4.2)$$

For example, in Figure 4.1, the price difference between point "A" to point "C" is the TMV in that trend, and the time that it takes to complete this trend is T.

Overall, in a DC-based summary, the financial data is first sampled by two types of events: a DC event, and an OS event, according to the value of the threshold. And secondly, a number of indicators are used to extract the trading information from these two events.

4.2.2 Detecting Regime Changes through HMM

Building on our previous work [46], the Hidden Markov Model (HMM) was employed to detect regime changes from a series of DC indicators. The idea was to use HMM to estimate the hidden and unobserved "states" from the input data. In our case, the values of the DC indicator R were used as input data to the HMM. The output of HMM was hidden states detected by the model. Our interpretation, which was supported by significant political events, was that different hidden states represent different market regimes [46].

As in our previous work [46], a two-state HMM was adopted in this study. It meant that the HMM will only infer two types of hidden states from the input data. And to help us compare the market regimes across different data sets, we label a market period with less fluctuation as "Regime 1", which is considered as a rather stable market period. Alternatively, a market period with more sharp rises or falls in the price is labelled as "Regime 2", which is considered as a more volatile market period.

4.2.3 Comparing Market Regimes in an Indicator Space

A market regime represents the behaviour of a market during a particular period of time. Market regimes across different financial markets may share similar characteristics with each other. For example, the Regime 1 of the UK stock market may have a similar performance to the Regime 1 of the US stock market. One way to compare and contrast market regimes of different financial markets is to position them in an indicator space. If the position of a market regime is close to another market regime in the indicator space, then one may conclude that they are similar to each other. Furthermore, by observing enough numbers of market regimes, one may be able to generalise where the normal regimes occupy in the indicator space.

Figure 4.2 depicts an example of being able to position market regimes in an indicator space. As mentioned above, the market regime is detected by adapting the HMM. And the input data of the model is the data of the DC-based indicator R, which is calculated by the other two DC-based indicators: TMV and T. Thus, a period of one market regime can also be described by two DC-based indicators: TMV and T. In Figure 4.2, a two-dimensional indicator space is constructed, where the x-axis measured the average value of T, and the y-axis measured an average value of TMV. The average T and average TMV can be measured in each period within a market regime. Each period therefore occupies one position in the indicator space. Five hypothetical periods of each regime are shown in Figure 4.2.

Market regimes detected in different financial markets may vary in their TMV and T. For example, in one market, the TMV could range between 1 and 6, but in another market, TMV could range between 1

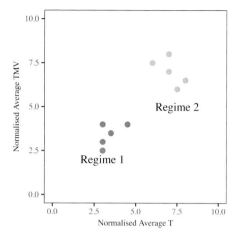

FIGURE 4.2: A hypothetical example of an indicator space.

and 8. To relate the results found in different markets, we normalise the values of the DC-indicators, before positioning them into the indicator space. An approach called "feature scaling" or "Min–Max scaling" is used here to normalise the range of the data [2]. With this approach, the data of the DC-based indicators is scaled to a fixed range between 0 and 1. The formula of normalisation is given as:

$$x' = \frac{x - min(x)}{max(x) - min(x)} \tag{4.3}$$

Here $max(x)$ and $min(x)$ refer to the maximum and minimum values within the observed data set for the particular market. For example, the maximum and minimum value of TMV and T were observed for the EUR–GBP exchange market over the period of data used, which were then used to normalise the values of TMV and T of each period. With data normalised, it is possible to retrospectively compare and contrast regimes from different markets.

4.3 EMPIRICAL STUDY

We then attempted to characterise what are normal and abnormal market regimes across different markets. To do so, we identify market regimes in different markets and in different periods. We compared the normal and abnormal regimes from different markets in the normalised indicator space. We wanted to see (a) whether normal regimes from different markets and different periods occupy similar positions in the normalised indicator space, and (b) whether positions occupied by normal regimes are separated from positions occupied by abnormal regimes across markets and time.

4.3.1 Data Sets

In order to characterise regimes across markets, ten different data sets were examined (see Table 4.1). The data sets are selected on both daily (low frequency) data and minute-by-minute (high-frequency) data. They covered three different asset types: stocks, commodities and foreign exchanges. The data was selected because it was related to four interesting market periods, where observable events took place (see the list below). During these periods of time, volatility in the financial markets changed abruptly, which indicated the possibility of observable regime changes in the markets.

1. The global financial crisis of 2007–2008.

2. The oil crash of 2014–2016.

3. The UK's European Union membership referendum in 2016.

4. The Chinese stock market turbulence of 2015–2016.

Table 4.1: Data sets.

Data	Daily Data		Minute-by-Minute Data	
	Financial Crisis 2007–2008	Oil Crash 2014–2016	Brexit 2016	Chinese Stock Market Turbulence 2015–2016
DJIA	√			
FTSE 100	√			
S&P 500	√			
Brent Oil		√		
WTI Oil		√		
EUR–GBP			√	
GBP–USD			√	
EUR–USD			√	
SSE				√
SZSE				√

For the study of the global financial crisis of 2007–2008, the closing price of three major stock indices was selected: Dow Jones Industrial Average Index (DJIA), FTSE 100 Index (FTSE 100) and S&P 500 Index (S&P 500). These three stock indices reflected the general trend of the US and the UK stock market.

For the study of the oil crash of 2014–2016, the price of two primary oil benchmarks were selected: the Brent Crude Oil and the WTI (West Texas Intermediate) Crude Oil. Oil prices significantly affect the cost of global industrial production. Brent Oil represents about two-thirds of oil traded around the world, while the WTI Oil is the benchmark for the oil price in the U.S [10].

For the study of the UK's EU referendum, three currency exchange rates were selected: Euro to British Pound (EUR–GBP), British Pound to US dollar (GBP–USD) and Euro to US dollar (EUR–USD). The British pound fluctuated against the euro and the dollar due to the uncertainty of the political events surrounding Brexit.

For the study of the turbulence in the Chinese stock market, two major stock market indices were selected: the Shanghai Stock Exchange Composite Index (SSE) and the Shenzhen Stock Exchange Component Index (SZSE). The Chinese indices were studied for comparison with the US and UK indices mentioned above.

We acknowledge that any time periods that we choose would have limitations. The selected data includes periods before, during and after major market events. This is because we want to see when regime changes would take place over periods of market uncertainty and fluctuation.

4.3.2 Summarising Data under DC

Under the DC approach, different observers may use different thresholds to sample prices. Here, for each data set, ten evenly distributed thresholds were applied to summarise the financial data: 0.1%, 0.2%, 0.3%, 0.4%, 0.5%, 0.6%, 0.7%, 0.8%, 0.9%, 1.0%. This meant that each data set was independently summarised with ten different thresholds. Thus, ten DC series were generated for each data set. With each DC series, values in three DC indicators were collected: TMV, T and R.

4.3.3 Detecting Regime Changes under HMM

As mentioned in Section 4.2.2, a two-state HMM was used for detecting regime changes. The values of the indicator R were fed into the HMM, which segmented the input period into two regimes: Regime 1 and Regime 2.

For the purpose of classifying the market regimes across different financial markets, the market regime that represented a stable period of time was labelled as Regime 1, or the normal regime, and the market regime that represented a more volatile period of time was labelled as Regime 2.

Extracted from [46], Figures 4.3 and 4.4 show examples of market regimes detected from the Brexit period. With the DC approach, the original price movement of the selected exchange rate, the euro against the US dollar (EUR–USD), is summarised into DC trends. Then market regimes were recognised through the HMM. The (short) time periods of Regime 2 were indicated in red shades, and the remainder of the time periods was recognised as Regime 1.

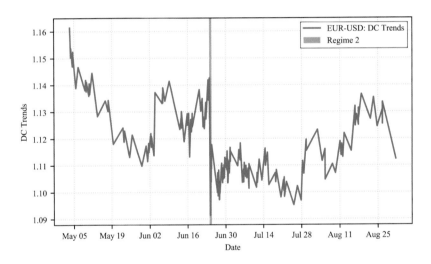

FIGURE 4.3: An example of recognition of market regimes. The DC trends of the exchange rate are presented in blue curves. The time periods of Regime 2 are indicated in red shades, and the remainder of the time periods is recognised as Regime 1.

4.3.4 Observing Market Regimes in the Normalised Indicator Space

In the previous step, market regimes are identified by the HMM. In order to compare and contrast different market regimes from different data sets, we placed the regimes on a DC indicator space. Earlier, we

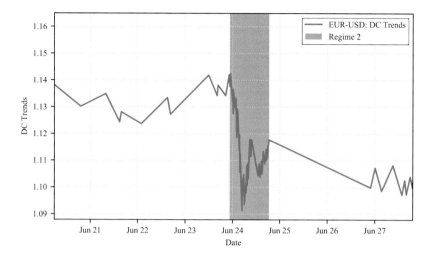

FIGURE 4.4: A zoomed-in version of the DC trends of EUR–USD.

mentioned that the HMM used the DC indicator R to detect regimes. Indicator R is computed by how much time it took (which is measured by T) to reach a certain level of price change (which is measured by TMV). We proposed to compare and contrast regimes with these raw measures, T and TMV. This would allow us to see more precisely how the two indicators interact and contribute to the differences between regimes.

A DC summary is a series of alternating uptrends and downtrends. HMM partitions the trends in this series into two regimes. A regime is a continuous sequence of trends in the DC summary. In a DC summary, we measure the T and TMV values of each trend [47]. After the trends are classified to be Regime 1 or Regime 2, we computed the average T and TMV values for the trends in each regime. Different markets and time periods may have had different norms in their T and TMV values. Therefore, to compare regimes from different markets, we normalised the T and TMV values as suggested in Equation 4.3 above.

The normalised average T and TMV values of each regime can be plotted onto a two-dimensional indicator space. Figure 4.5 shows an example of the positions of two market regimes in this two-dimensional space. In this example, trends in Regime 1 had a normalised average T value of 3 and a normalised average TMV value of 3. Regime 2, on the other hand, had a normalised average T and TMV values of 7 and 7, respectively.

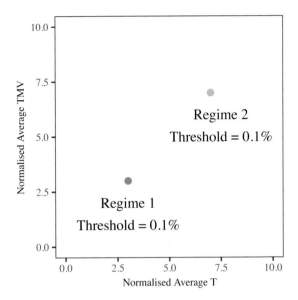

FIGURE 4.5: An example of describing market regimes in an indicator space.

By visualising the positions of the regimes in this indicator space, we aim to observe similarities and dissimilarities between different market regimes in different data sets, with the hope to be able to discover regularities.

4.4 RESULTS AND DISCUSSIONS

So far, we have explained that under a given threshold, DC summarised a data set into trends. HMM classified these trends into regimes, with each regime comprising a sequence of trends. Each trend defined a TMV and a T value. We computed the average TMV and average T values for each regime in each data set. In this section, we compared the normalised TMV and T values of the two regimes, from different markets and time periods.

For each data set, we computed the average TMV and T values for all the trends of each regime. For example, we computed the average normalised TMV and T values of all trends in Regime 1 in the data of GBP–USD, which is summarised under the threshold 0.1%, and the same is done for Regime 2. Each market regime in each data set will occupy a position within the two-dimensional (**T-TMV**) indicator space. This will allow us to see whether Regimes 1 and 2 occupy different regions of the indicator space. If they do, then it is possible to define the region of normal regime and abnormal regime.

4.4.1 Market Regimes in the Indicator Space

Figure 4.6 shows the positions of the regimes from all data sets on the T-TMV indicator space. They are grouped by their periods as shown in Table 4.1. To recap, the x-axis measures the normalised average value of the indicator T, and the y-axis measures the normalised average value of the indicator TMV. Each point in the indicator space shows the position of one market regime of one data set. The red points showed the positions of Regime 1, and the blue points showed the positions of Regime 2. For example, one of the red points in Figure 4.6(a) would show the average normalised TMV and T values of all trends in Regime 1 in GBP–USD summarised under the threshold 0.1%.

In Figure 4.6, we studied the market regimes found in the four market events separately: (a) market regimes from the data of Brexit; (b) market regimes from the data of Chinese stock market turbulence of 2015–2016; (c) market regimes from the (three) data sets of the financial crisis of 2007–2008; (d) market regimes from the (two) data sets of the oil crash of 2014–2016.

As we examined three foreign exchange pairs (EUR–USD, EUR–GBP and GBP–USD) and each data set is summarised with ten thresholds, there are 30 data points for each regime in Figure 4.6(a). As we used two Chinese indices (SSE and SZSE) and ten thresholds per data set, there are 20 data points for each regime in Figure 4.6(b). There are 30 and 20 data points per regime for Figures 4.6(c) and (d), respectively.

Figure 4.6 clearly shows that, within each group, Regime 1 and Regime 2 are clearly separable in the T-TMV indicator space. For example, Figure 4.6(a) shows that, compared to Regime 1, Regime 2 takes a much shorter time than normal to complete (readers are reminded that the x-axis represents normalised T, not absolute T). Figure 4.6(a) shows that Regime 2 has a much higher (normalised) TMV to (normalised) T ratio. The same is observed in Figures 4.6(b), (c) and (d).

Distribution of the regimes in the normalised T-TMV space is also significant: the market regimes that occurred from the data taken from the events of Brexit and that of the Chinese stock market turbulence were linearly distributed. But the market regimes from the data of the financial crisis and the oil crash formed clusters. The obvious difference between these data sets is that high-frequency (minute-to-minute) data was used for the former, and low frequency (daily) data was used for the latter. Having said that, the exact reason for these differences in distributions demands further investigation; this will be left to future research.

In general, Regime 2 suggests a market with higher TMV to (normalised) T ratio. This means, given the same T, Regime 2 tends to have a larger TMV than Regime 1. Given the same TMV, Regime 2 tends to have a smaller T than Regime 1. As pointed out by [47], both larger TMV and smaller T are indicators of higher volatility. Therefore, one could roughly understand Regime 2 as a regime that represents periods of higher volatility.

Figure 4.7 shows the market regimes of all the data sets together in one indicator space. We can see from Figure 4.7 that the positions of Regime 1 and Regime 2 are largely separable, with some exceptions around (0.11, 0.16). Figure 4.7 suggests that, across asset types, time and thresholds, Regimes 1 and 2 occupy different areas in the normalised T-TMV indicator space.

4.4.2 Market Regimes under Different Thresholds

When summarising data with DC, different observers may use different thresholds. The question is: are the positions of the regimes sensitive to the thresholds used? To be able to answer that, we analyse the market regimes observed under different thresholds.

Figure 4.8 depicts the market regimes in the normalised T-TMV indicator space with regard to different values of thresholds. It shows that positions of the market regimes are changing along with the value of thresholds in some data sets, but not all of them. For instance, in Figures 4.8 a and b, the market regimes with larger price movements (indicator TMV) are captured under larger thresholds, even after normalisation.

However, Figures 4.8 c and d show a different picture. Data points collected from different thresholds mingled. This suggested that the size of threshold has little effect on the T-TMV positions of the market regimes in these two data sets.

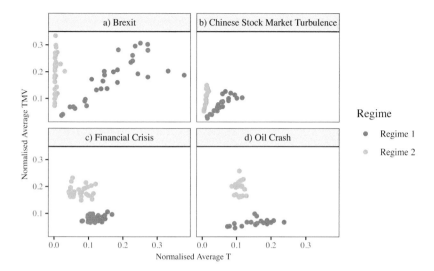

FIGURE 4.6: (a)–(d) Market regimes in the indicator space, which are organised by four market events: (a) market regimes from the data of Brexit, (b) market regimes from the data of Chinese stock market turbulence, (c) market regimes from the data of the financial crisis, (d) market regimes from the data of the oil crash.

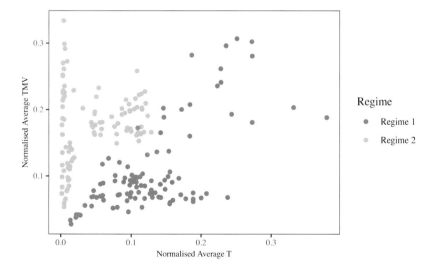

FIGURE 4.7: Indicator space of all data sets.

For reference, Figure 4.9 shows the regimes from all data sets. Obviously, the positions of the regimes are the same as those shown in Figure 4.7. Figure 4.9 gives an idea of the thresholds which are generated from the different regimes.

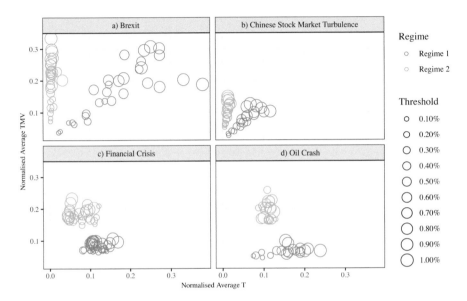

FIGURE 4.8: (a)–(d) Market regimes in the indicator space with regards to different values of thresholds.

4.4.3 Discussion

In this section, we highlight some of the major points made in this chapter. Firstly, we have demonstrated that the DC indicator space is useful for comparing different markets. By positioning the market regimes in the DC indicator space, the distance between different regimes can be measured. This allows us to quantitatively measure the distance between different regimes in different markets. We can determine whether regimes are different or similar to each other, in terms of their positions in the indicator space.

Secondly, the position of the market regimes allows us to classify different types of the market regimes. We have found that all the Regime 1's are similar to each other across assets, markets and time. All of the Regime 2's are similar to each other. But Regime 1's and Regime 2's occupy different positions within the DC indicator space. As shown

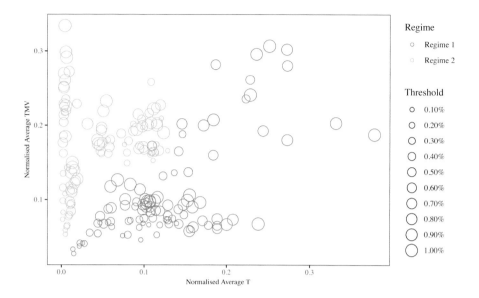

FIGURE 4.9: Indicator space of all data sets with regards to different value of thresholds.

in Figure 4.8, the two regimes are clearly separable in each of the four markets studied. Even when we put the regimes found in different markets together, Regime 1's and Regime 2's are separable, with a little amount of overlap (see Figure 4.9). The overlap is mainly due to regimes found in the oil crash market (2014–2016). This could suggest that the commodity market is slightly different from the stock and foreign exchange market; this is a much bigger topic which will be left for future research.

Thirdly, by observing the positions of the market regimes, it is possible to define the region of normal market and the abnormal market in the indicator space. We called them normal and abnormal because in all the periods that we chose, dramatic external events took place, for example the bank failures in the 2007–2008 global financial crisis or the shock result of the Brexit referendum in Britain in 2016, all of which affected financial markets. In all our observations, the market changed from Regime 1 (which experienced less volatility) to Regime 2 (higher volatility) around these events. It is reasonable to believe that the regime change was either an anticipation, or a reaction, to these unpredictable events. For convenience, we have described what has happened when the markets changed from a normal regime to an abnormal regime.

Let us elaborate our findings by looking more closely into the results. We say that the market experienced less volatility in Regime 1, the normal market. This can be seen in Figures 4.6 a and b, where less time (indicator T) is required to complete a similar amount of price movements (indicator TMV) in Regime 2, than that of in Regime 1. And in Figures 4.6 c and d, less price movements are achieved within a similar amount of time when the market was in Regime 1, compared to the market periods in Regime 2. This indicated that Regime 1 represented a less volatile market period.

On the other hand, we say that the market experienced higher volatility in Regime 2, the abnormal market. This can be seen in Figures 4.6 a and b, where bigger price movements were observed within a shorter period of time, in the region of Regime 2, than those in the region of Regime 1. In Figures 4.6 c and d, bigger price movements (TMV) were completed in Regime 2, than those completed in Regime 1, within a similar amount of time (T). These indicated that Regime 2 represented a higher level of market volatility.

We note that the choice of threshold affected the positions of the markets on the indicator space in some markets but not others. But overall, independent of the thresholds used, the two regimes occupy different areas of the DC indicator space. The relative positions of the normal and abnormal regimes are insensitive to the thresholds used, which indicated that our research is correct, that thresholds do not influence the outcome of regime positions.

Finally, it is worth clarifying that our aim is not about finding the "optimal" threshold for regime clarification. The intention was to generalise DC characteristics of normal regimes. That is why various thresholds are used to find normal regimes, and their results are used together to characterise normal regimes. Figures 4.8 c and d show that the same regimes found under different thresholds mingle with each other.

4.5 CONCLUSIONS

In the previous research chapter (Chapter 3), an approach was established as to how to recognise regime changes using market data; the approach was to summarise raw data as trends under DC [29]. Following [47], we collected values of the DC indicator R (which measures return) for each trend. The series of R was fed into a Hidden Markov Model (HMM), which classified trends into two regimes. In other words, the market is partitioned into periods of two regimes, classified by us as normal and abnormal.

The purpose of this chapter is to characterise normal and abnormal market regimes. To achieve this, a new way is proposed to compare, contrast and classify different market regimes. We have applied the approach that has been developed in Chapter 3 to more data: ten different assets were selected from four market periods during which significant events took place (see Table 4.1). For generalisation over data frequency, we used both low frequency (daily closing prices) and high-frequency (minute-by-minute closing price) data of different types (stocks, foreign exchange and commodities).

The proposed method [46] was applied to detect regime changes in each of the 10 market periods. To enable us to compare and contrast results across market periods, we labelled the regime with lower R values as Regime 1, and the regime with higher R values as Regime 2 in each market period. We call Regime 1 the normal market periods and Regime 2 the abnormal market periods, because the latter always took place after significant events occurred in our research. The market typically returned to and stayed in Regime 1 afterwards.

We profiled each regime detected with the two DC indicators that define R: TMV (price changes in a trend) and T (time). This allowed us to plot each regime onto a two-dimensional DC-indicator space. The plottings enabled us to see that the two regimes were clearly separable within each group of data sets (see Figure 4.6). Plotting the results of all data sets together suggested that the two regimes are reasonably separable (see Figure 4.7). In other words, similarities were found between regimes across different asset types, time, data frequencies and thresholds. This was a significant discovery: it suggested that the TMV and T values of the last trend (and the current, unfinished trend) could potentially be used to monitor the market, to see whether regime change transition is taking place. This would have implications for risk assessment and selection of trading strategies. This would be discussed in the next chapter.

To summarise, this is the first attempt to establish statistical properties of normal and abnormal regimes in terms of their positions in the DC indicators space, under the DC framework. These properties hold across asset types, time, data frequencies and thresholds. Being able to characterise normal regimes opens doors for future research in monitoring regime changes. For example, if the market is moving away from the normal regime to an abnormal regime, a trader may consider closing their position or adopting a different trading strategy. Market monitoring and trading will be left for future research.

CHAPTER 5

Tracking Regime Changes Using Directional Change Indicators

In the previous chapters, we showed that regime changes in the market are retrospectively detectable using historic data under Directional Change (DC). In this chapter, we build on such results and show that how the DC indicators can be used for market tracking, using data up to the present, to understand what is going on in the market. In particular, we want to track the market to see whether it is entering an abnormally volatile regime.

The proposed approach used the values of DC indicators that were observed in the past to model the normal regime of a market (in which volatility is normal) or an abnormal regime (in which volatility is abnormally high). Given a particular value observed in the current market, we used a Naïve Bayes classifier to calculate independently two probabilities: one for the market being in the normal regime, and one for it being in the abnormal regime. Both the two probabilities were combined to decide which regime the market should be in. To achieve this purpose, two decision rules are examined: a Simple Rule and a Stricter Rule.

In this chapter, three sets of stock indices are used to examine the proposed approach. They are the DJIA, FTSE 100 and S&P 500. We use the daily closing price from 2007 to 2009 to build the model. Then the model is used to track regime changes for each index individually from 2010 to 2012.

The results suggest that the tracking method presented in this chapter, with either decision rule, managed to pick up spells of regime changes accurately. That means the tracking signals could be useful to market participants. This study potentially lays the foundation of a practical financial early warning system.

This chapter is organised as follows: Section 5.1 discusses the purpose of this chapter. Section 5.2 elaborates the proposed methodology for tracking regime changes. The empirical results are analysed and discussed in Section 5.4. Section 5.5 concludes this chapter.

5.1 INTRODUCTION

In our previous work, we proposed an approach to detect regime changes. The empirical results showed that the detected regime changes coincided with a significant market event, the UK's referendum on Brexit in June 2016. Our work proved that the fluctuation of the financial market could be detected and summarised as regime changes, in other words moving from one regime to another. However, such regime changes were detected in hindsight. The question in this chapter is whether one could use the information up to the present time to track regime changes, as they occur in real time.

In Chapter 3, we classified markets into two regimes. We named the regime with higher volatility the "abnormal regime", as it emerged after a significant event (namely, the Brexit referendum) had taken place. In a subsequent work, in Chapter 4, we applied the same method to different financial markets [19]. We found that the two regimes have unique characteristics. In other words, we can characterise normal and abnormal regimes across different financial markets.

However, in both Chapters 3 and 4, regimes were detected retrospectively. In this chapter, we will explain how one could use data up to the present to track the market, with the aim to recognise regime changes, preferably without too much delay.

The tracking method proposed can be divided into two steps: first, we use a machine learning model, a Naïve Bayes classifier to compute the probability of the market being in the normal or abnormal regime, respectively, based on (i) the market data observed up to the present; and (ii) characteristics of the past regimes observed across markets (in

Chapter 4). Second, the two computed probabilities are combined to form a final classification on which regime the market is currently in.

The method proposed in this chapter monitored the market as prices changed. Thus, it could be employed as a warning system, alerting market participants of likely regime changes. How traders and regulators may act upon such information is beyond the scope of this chapter. It is also important to clarify that in this chapter, we purely focus on what the data up to now tells us about the market, i.e, it is purely data-led. No forecasting is attempted.

5.2 METHODOLOGY

In this section, we propose a method for tracking price movements dynamically with the aim to detect what are the likely regime changes in the market. An illustration of the proposed method for regime changes tracking is provided in Figure 5.1. The idea is to observe the DC indicator TMV and T in the current trend, and compare these values to those found in the normal regimes indicated in the past [19]. A Naïve Bayes classifier is applied to compute two probabilities independently: (i) the probability of the market being in the normal regime, and (ii) the probability of the market being in the abnormal regime. These two probabilities are combined to conclude what regime the market is currently in – two decision methods will be proposed below.

5.2.1 Tracking DC Trends

Summarising the financial data into DC trends using the DC approach enabled us to focus on what are the significant price changes. However, according to the definition of DC [44], one DC trend will not be confirmed until the next DC event is triggered. This may cause a delay when tracking regime changes based on DC trends. Therefore, a dynamic way is required to track the DC trends to take the research further.

Figure 5.2 explains what tracking means in this chapter. At every time point i, the values of $TMV(i)$ and $T(i)$ are calculated. With the help of past data, one attempts to infer from these values whether the market is in or out of the normal regime at time i. It is important to note that tracking uses data up to now. For example, the last known extreme point at time 10 is Point A at time 4, because point C is not confirmed as an extreme point until time 11 (when the price drops

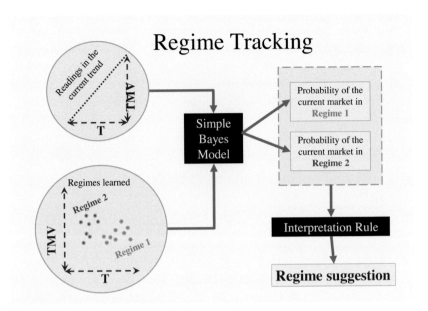

FIGURE 5.1: An illustration of regime tracking.

from point C by θ). Therefore, $TMV(10)$ should be calculated with the price at point A as P_{EXT_i}; $T(10)$ should be calculated with the time at point A as T_{EXT_i}.

5.2.2   Use of a Naïve Bayes Classifier

In Chapter 4, we have shown how to characterise normal and abnormal regimes. Here, given the value of tracked TMV and T in the on-going trend, we can compare their values with those observed in normal and abnormal regimes in the past (which we refer to as training data) to calculate the probability of the current market being in either regime. For that, we employ the use of a Naïve Bayes Classifier (NBC).

The NBC is an algorithm for the classification task. It allows us to track the on-going regime changes based on the information of regime changes in the past. In order to do that, the classifier needs to be trained with historical data. This section explains how this can be done.

In statistics, the Bayes' theorem is used to describe the probability of an event, based on prior knowledge of conditions that might be related to the event. Based on the Bayes' theorem, the NBC allows us to calculate the conditional probability of the current market being

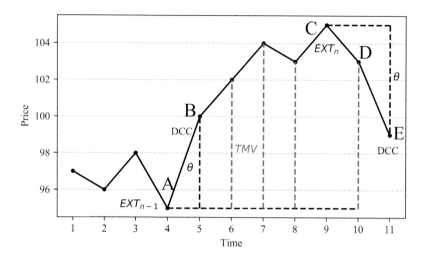

FIGURE 5.2: A hypothetical example of tracking the unfinished DC trends.

in a particular regime, based on the information of previous regime changes. Using Bayes' theorem, the NBC is established as follows:

$$p(C_k|x) = \frac{p(C_k)p(x|C_k)}{p(x)}, \tag{5.1}$$

where $p(C_k)$ is the prior probability of class k, $p(x|C_k)$ is the conditional probability of each input data given the class label, and $p(x)$ is the prior probability of the data.

Classification using the NBC includes two phases: the training phase and the testing phase. In the training phase, the model is trained with a training data set, which is a set of data that associated with class labels. In the testing phase, the model is applied to classify the test data set in which the class label is unknown.

To train an NBC with a given data set, the parameters of the model need to be estimated. The prior probability of the class $p(C_k)$ represents the probability of the occurrence of the market regimes are in the training data set. Since only two types of market regimes are considered in this book, $p(C_1)$ and $p(C_2)$ represent the probability of the market being in Regime 1 and Regime 2, respectively.

The conditional probability $P(x|C_k)$ represents the probability of seeing the input variable x when it is known to belong to regime C_k.

Suppose we have two input features, which can be represented by x_1 and x_2. Then the conditional probability can be calculated as:

$$p(x|C_k) = p(x_1|C)p(x_2|C) \tag{5.2}$$

As discussed in Section 5.2.1, the input feature of the NBC is a sequence of two DC indicators: TMV and T. It can be written as $x_i = (TMV_i, T_i)$, depicting i measured values.

Since our input variables are continuous data, we typically assume the variable x follows a Gaussian distribution with a mean μ and standard deviation σ. Then by estimating the density function of the distribution, the probability $p(x|C_k)$ can be calculated:

$$p(x|C_k) = \frac{1}{\sqrt{2\pi\sigma_k^2}} exp\left(-\frac{(x-\mu_k)^2}{2\sigma_k^2}\right), \tag{5.3}$$

where μ_k and σ_k represent the mean and the standard deviation of the input feature x in class k. These values are learnt from the training data. For example, suppose the training data contains a continuous variable, x. We first segment the data by the class (regime), and then compute the mean and variance of x for each regime.

With the estimated distribution, the probability $p(x|C_k)$ can be calculated given new data. For example, suppose we have collected some new observations v from the test data set. The probability $p(x|C_k)$ can be computed by plugging v into Equation 5.3, which is a Gaussian distribution parametrized by μ_k and σ_k. That is:

$$p(x = v|C_k) = \frac{1}{\sqrt{2\pi\sigma_k^2}} exp\left(-\frac{(v-\mu_k)^2}{2\sigma_k^2}\right). \tag{5.4}$$

The last component that needs to be calculated in the NBC is the prior probability of input variable $p(x)$. It is the marginal probability that an input feature x is seen, regardless of whether the market is in either regime, which can be calculated as:

$$p(x) = p(x|C_1)p(C_1) + p(x|C_2)p(C_2) \tag{5.5}$$

Now, the NBC is trained by learning the parameters from the training data. Given the training data with observation of the input features and the associated class of regimes, the classifier can be established. With it, given the test data, the probability that each data belongs to a particular regime can be calculated. Algorithm 1 explains how to train an NBC and apply it to the test data.

Algorithm 1 Naïve Bayes Classifier

Training Phase
Input: Training Data (x, C)
Output: Parameters of the Model
1. Calculate the prior probability of class, $p(C_k)$.
2. Calculate the mean μ_k and the standard deviation σ_k of the input feature of each class.
3. Estimate the Gaussian distribution of each class $p(x|C_k)$.
4. Calculate prior probability of the input feature, $p(x)$.

Testing Phase
Input: Test Data (v)
Output: The probability $p(C_k|x = v)$
1. For each observation in v, plugging it into the Gaussian distribution parametrized by μ_k and σ_k.
2. Calculate the probability $p(x = v|C_k)$.
3. Calculate the probability $p(C_k|x = v)$.

5.3 EXPERIMENT SETUP

5.3.1 Data

The empirical study of this chapter focuses on three stock indices: the Dow Jones Industrial Average (DJIA), the FTSE 100, and the S&P 500. These stock indices were chosen because they were linked to the 2007–2008 global financial crisis, where regime changes were considered to have taken place in financial markets. For each index, the daily closing price is recorded from January 2007 to December 2012 to cover periods of the financial crisis.

To examine the proposed method, the data set was separated into two data sets: training data sets and test data sets (see Table 5.1). For each data set, the data sampled from January 2007 to December 2009 is considered as the training data. And the data sampled from January 2010 to December 2012 is considered as the test data. The parameters of the NBC were estimated from the training data sets. Then the model was used to detect regime changes on the test data set. For example, to track regime change on the Dow Jones Index, the NBC is first trained on the training data of the Dow Jones index. It is then used to track regime changes on the test data of the Dow Jones index.

In the training data sets, the raw financial data is summarised into

Table 5.1: Time periods of training and test data set.

Data Set	Time Periods	
	Training Periods	**Test Periods**
DJIA	03/01/2007–31/12/2009	01/01/2010–28/12/2012
FTSE 100	03/01/2007–31/12/2009	01/01/2010–28/12/2012
S&P 500	03/01/2007–31/12/2009	01/01/2010–28/12/2012

completed DC trends, under a threshold of 0.3%. The DC trends are then measured by two DC indicators: TMV_{EXT} and T_{EXT}. This is because on the basis of the regime change detection approach proposed in Chapter 3, the value of the completed DC trends are used to detect regime changes. Therefore, these values are used to detect regime changes and train the NBC.

On the other hand, in the test data sets, the raw financial data was summarised in the on going DC trends, which were then measured by two DC indicators TMV and T. As discussed in Section 5.2.1, their values were used to track the market. In Chapter 4, we showed that the two regimes were clearly separable on the TMV-T space when both TMV and T are normalised. Therefore, the training and test data were both normalised before modelling by the NBC. The data was normalised using the min–max normalisation approach.

In the empirical study, the parameters of the NBC are learnt from the training data sets. And the model is used to recognise market regimes for each pair of input features from the test data sets.

5.3.2 Regime Changes on the Data

With the benefit of hindsight, regime changes can be detected on each data set using the method that we proposed in Chapter 3. Figure 5.3 to Figure 5.5 show the detected regimes on each stock index, respectively. These figures are produced for demonstrating the status of the market in terms of regime changes over the whole chosen time period.

5.4 EMPIRICAL RESULTS

In this section, we will analyse the effectiveness of the NBC and the two decision rules. The purpose of this analysis is to investigate whether the proposed method is able to track regime changes on the test data sets.

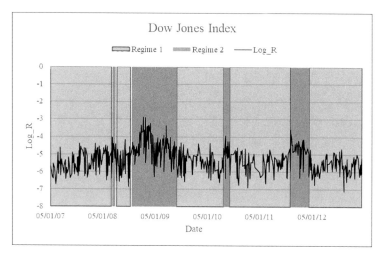

FIGURE 5.3: Regime changes on the DJIA Index.

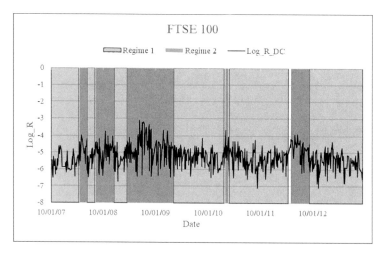

FIGURE 5.4: Regime changes on the FTSE 100 Index.

The NBC is established with observations on the training data sets. The model is then used to monitor the market, by calculating the probabilities of the market being in the two regimes, $p(C_1|x)$ and $p(C_2|x)$, for each data set from the test data sets. With the probabilities calculated, we attempt to combine them and determine which regime the current market belongs to. For this purpose, two decision rules are designed and compared. The regimes classified by these rules are compared with the regimes computed by the method presented in

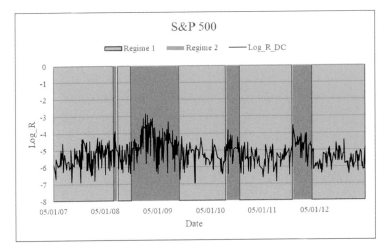

FIGURE 5.5: Regime changes on the S&P 500 Index.

Chapter 3. This comparison allows us to assess the performance of our classification approach.

5.4.1 Calculating Probability

As discussed in Section 5.2.2, the conditional probability of the occurrence of the current market, given the TMV and T values in the current trend, can be calculated by the NBC. Figure 5.6 shows the calculated probabilities of the market belonging to Regime 1 (the normal regime) and to Regime 2 (the abnormal regime), $p(C_1|x)$ and $p(C_2|x)$, over time. A higher $p(C_1|x)$ value means the market is more likely to be in the normal regime; similarly, a higher $p(C_2|x)$ means the higher likelihood that the current market is in the abnormal regime. For instance, as shown in Figure 5.6, from the mid-2011 to early 2012, the probabilities of being in Regime 2 are much higher than that of being in Regime 1 on the Dow Jones index. This may imply that the market fell into Regime 2 in that period. The estimated probabilities for the FTSE 100 index and the S&P 500 index are shown in Figure 5.7, and Figure 5.8.

For each (TMV, T) pair, two probabilities are calculated independently. For $p(C_1|x)$ and $p(C_2|x)$ to be useful, we need to combine them in order to decide whether the market is in Regime 1 or Regime 2. For this purpose, two decision rules are proposed in the next sections.

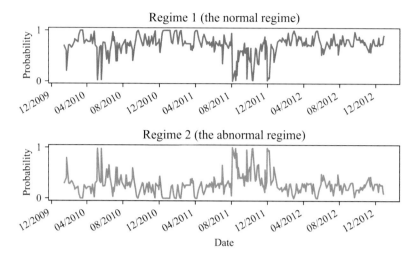

FIGURE 5.6: Estimated probabilities for the Dow Jones Index. The blue line indicates the probability of the market being in Regime 1, $p(C_1|x)$, and the orange line indicates the probability of the market being in Regime 2, $p(C_1|x)$.

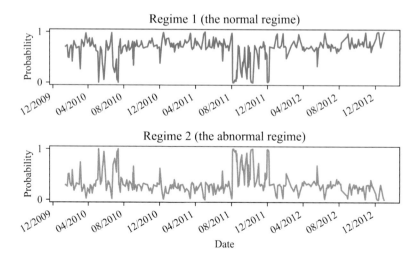

FIGURE 5.7: Estimated probabilities for the FTSE 100 Index.

5.4.2 B-Simple for Regime Classification

The NBC compared each (TMV, T) pair with those found in the training data, and calculated the probabilities of the market belonging to

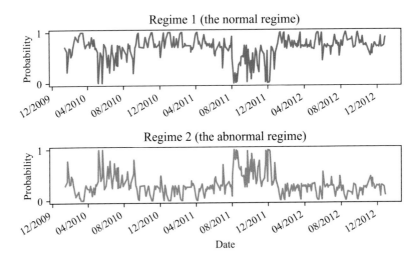

FIGURE 5.8: Estimated probabilities for the S&P 500 Index.

Regime 1 and Regime 2 independently. A Simple Rule is where the hypothesis picked is most probable. In our case, it meant choosing the regime with the highest probability:

$$
\begin{aligned}
&\text{choose } C_1 \quad \text{if } p(C_1|x) > p(C_2|x) \\
&\text{choose } C_2 \quad \text{if } p(C_2|x) > p(C_1|x),
\end{aligned}
\tag{5.6}
$$

where C_1 and C_2 represent Regime 1 and Regime 2, $p(C_1|x)$ and $p(C_2|x)$ denote the probabilities of the market belonging to Regime 1 and Regime 2, respectively. We call this approach that combined the NBC with the Simple Rule: B-Simple.

5.4.3 B-Strict for Regime Classification

As discussed in the previous section, some false alarms are reported in the mentioned regimes, with B-Simple (see the Simple Rules defined in Equation 5.6). If we want to reduce false alarms, we could combine the outcome probability of the NBC with a stricter classification rule. What makes up the designed stricter decision rule is made up as follows:

$$
\begin{aligned}
&\text{choose } C_1 \quad \text{if } p(C_1|x) > p(C_2|x) \\
&\text{choose } C_2 \quad \text{if } p(C_2|x) > p(C_1|x) \text{ and } p(C_2|x) > threshold_2,
\end{aligned}
\tag{5.7}
$$

where C_1 and C_2 represent Regime 1 and Regime 2, $p(C_1|x)$ and $p(C_2|x)$ denote the probabilities of the market belonging to Regime 1 and Regime 2, respectively. Here $threshold_2$ is the lower bound value of $p(C_2|x)$ for the market to be concluded in Regime 2. The value of $threshold_2$ is a parameter defined by investors, reflecting its cautiousness of concluding Regime 2. In this chapter, the $threshold_2$ value was set to 0.8. The Stricter Rule is exactly the same as the Simple Rule, except that a minimal probability of $p(C_2|x)$ must be observed before concluding Regime 2. We call the method of combining the NBC with the stricter rule: B-Strict. Also, B-Simple can be seen as a special case of B-Strict, where one sets the threshold to 0.5.

5.4.4 Tracked Regime Changes

This section explains the empirical results. Figure 5.9 to Figure 5.11 compares the actual regime changes with the performance of the tracked regime changes. In each figure, the actual regime is shown on the top, which is detected using the method that was proposed in Chapter 3. The regime classification using B-Simple is shown in the middle, and the regime classification using B-Strict is shown at the bottom. They are both measured using the method that is proposed in Section 5.2.

5.4.4.1 Tracked Regime Changes on DJIA Index

Figure 5.9 compares the actual regimes and the tracked regime on the Dow Jones index. The top figure shows the market regimes computed by the method proposed in Chapter 3; we call them the actual regimes as they were computed with the benefit of hindsight. The middle figure shows the regime classification using B-Simple and the bottom figure shows the regime classification using B-Strict.

By comparing the actual regimes and the tracked regimes, we can tell the performance of regime tracking mechanism. The key issue to observe is: does the tracking mechanism have the ability to detect Regime 2 when it happened? If so, how long does it take the tracking mechanism to realise regime change has occurred after it has taken place?

The actual regimes indicate that the index experienced two spells of regime changes. The first spell of Regime 2 is recognized from 27

April 2010 to 7 June 2010, and the second one is found from 8 August 2011 to 14 December 2011.

Firstly, two spells of Regime 2 are detected by using both B-Simple and B-Strict. This means, by using data up to the time when regime classification is made, both B-Simple and B-Strict can detect Regime 2 when it took place. As tracking does not have the benefit of hindsight, it is reasonable to expect delay: in other words, it may take some time before the tracking mechanism realised that regime change has taken place.

By using B-Simple, the first signal of Regime 2 is spotted on 22/01/2010, which can be considered as a false alarm. The second signal is found on 06/05/2010, nine days later than actual regime changes took place. This is not a bad outcome, because the actual regime changes were computed with the benefit of hindsight. The tracking method proposed here lets the data tell us what happens in the market: no forecasting is attempted.

However, in the second period of Regime 2, B-Simple suggested that regime change occurred ahead of the actual change. The actual regime changes took place from 08/08/2011 to 14/12/2011. B-Simple suggested Regime 2 took place on 04/08/2011, four days ahead of the actual regime change. This is possibly because in Chapter 3, regime changes are computed based on completed trends. In tracking, we are dealing with the on-going trends. Therefore, when the TMV value goes sufficiently high within a short time, Regime 2 could have been concluded.

The second point to note is that B-Simple raised the alarm of regime change repeatedly, as opposed to raising persistent alarms throughout the Regime 2 spell. This is understandable because the method proposed in Chapter 3 attempted to model the Hidden Markov state, which carried a momentum. In B-Simple, only the current (TMV, T) reading is used for decision making. Besides, in practice, traders could react when such an alarm is first raised. So, the alarms raised by B-Simple do not have to be persistent to be useful to users. Repeated alarms would simply reinforce the message.

On the other hand, by using B-Strict, the first spell of Regime 2 is found on 06/05/2010, the same as the observation under B-Simple. For the second spell of Regime 2, the closest signals of Regime 2 are found on 04/08/2011, which are also the same as the findings under B-Simple. As shown in Figure 5.9, B-Strict is able to track regime changes but with less repeated alarms.

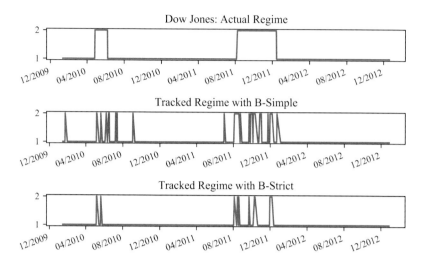

FIGURE 5.9: Comparison between actual regimes and tracked regimes on the DJIA Index.

5.4.4.2 Tracked Regime Changes on FTSE 100 Index

Figure 5.10 compares the actual regimes and the tracked regime on the FTSE 100 index. As shown in the top chart, two spells of Regime 2 are observed on FTSE 100 index. The first one ranges from 07/05/2010 to 27/05/2010, and the second one ranges from 08/08/2011 to 14/12/2011.

Under B-Simple, the signal for the first spell of Regime 2 is found on 05/05/2010, two days ahead of the actual regime change took place. For second spell of Regime 2, the signal is found on 04/08/2011, four days in advance. Here, B-Simple reports a number of repeated alarms, but some of them should be considered as false alarms (does not match the actual regimes).

Under B-Strict, the first spell of Regime is found on 06/05/2010, one day ahead of the actual regime change. And for the second spell of Regime 2, the signal is also found on 04/08/2011, four days ahead of the actual regime change.

Apart from that, B-Strict also raises alarms repeatedly (as opposed to continuously) during the Regime 2 spells, but it raises fewer alarms than B-Simple. As explained above, this does not prevent B-Strict from being useful to market participants.

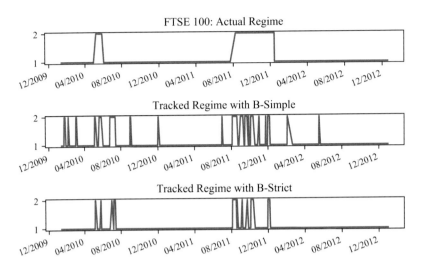

FIGURE 5.10: Comparison between actual regimes and tracked regimes on the FTSE 100 Index.

5.4.4.3 Tracked Regime Changes on S&P 500

Figure 5.11 compares the actual regimes and the tracked regimes on the S&P 500 index. As shown in the chart, the actual Regime 2 took place on two periods: from 27/04/2010 to 26/07/2010, and from 08/08/2011 to 14/12/2011.

Under B-Simple, the first spell of Regime 2 is tracked on 06/05/2010, nine days behind the first spell of the actual Regime 2. In the second spell of Regime 2, the tracked Regime 2 is recognised on 02/08/2011, six days ahead of the actual regime changes.

Under B-Strict, the tracked Regime 2 is found on 06/05/2010, the same as using the B-Simple rule. The second spell of Regime 2 is found on 08/08/2011, exactly the day when the actual regime change took place.

5.4.5 Discussion

To examine the proposed regime change tracking method, three data sets are used to test the tracking mechanism. Table 5.2 shows the time lag between the actual regimes and the tracked regimes. Table 5.3 shows the number of alarms that are raised by different decision rules.

Here, we focus on the ability of the decision rules to pick up Regime

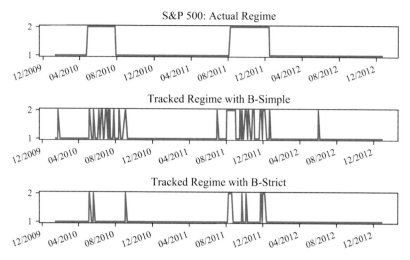

FIGURE 5.11: Comparison between actual regimes and tracked regimes on the S&P 500 Index.

2. This is because market participants are likely to benefit from alarms being registered when the market moved into a volatile regime, which is what Regime 2 represents.

In Table 5.2, the positive number tells the number of days that the tracked regimes are behind the actual regimes, where the negative number tells the number of days that the tracked regimes are ahead of the actual regimes.

As can be seen in Table 5.2, we can conclude that: first, two decision rules are managed to pick up regime changes as they happened. While two spells of regime changes are appeared in the test periods, they are all picked up by the rules. That means the decision rules are useful to market participants.

Second, the decision rules are likely to report regime changes earlier than the actual regime changes that happened. As shown in Table 5.2, 8 out of 12 alarms are raised ahead of or spot on the actual regime changes. Such results are positive. That means our tracking mechanism is likely to raise the alarm of regime changes in advance.

Third, as shown in Figure 5.9 to Figure 5.11, more alarms are raised using the B-Simple rule than using the B-Strict rule. This indicates that the simple rule intends to raise alarms repeatedly. But by setting the threshold in the B-Strict rule, fewer alarms would be raised.

Fourth, the number of true alarms and false alarms under the two decision rules is compared in Table 5.3. A true alarm is an alarm raised when the market is actually in Regime 2. The result shows that first, much more alarms (both true and false alarms) are generated by the B-Simple rule than by the B-Strict rule. Second, fewer false alarms are generated by the B-Strict rule than by the B-Simple rule. Third, the number of false alarms generated by the B-Simple rule is not excessive. Thus, we consider that both rules are useable. Which rule a market participant might prefer depends on the market participant's attitude towards the false alarms and how the signals are used.

Table 5.2: Tracked regime under different decision rules.

Data Set	B-Simple		B-Strict	
	1st Spell	2nd Spell	1st Spell	2nd Spell
DJIA	+9	-4	+9	-4
FTSE 100	-2	-4	-1	-4
S&P 500	+9	-6	+9	0

Table 5.3: Alarms raised under different decision rules.

Data Set	B-Simple		B-Strict	
	True Alarm	False Alarm	True Alarm	False Alarm
DJIA	23	11	12	1
FTSE 100	31	22	18	8
S&P 500	35	19	16	1
Total	89	52	46	10

5.5 CONCLUSION

In Chapter 3 we presented a way to detect regime changes in hindsight. In Chapter 4 we showed that normal regimes share similar characteristics – in their normalised TMV and T values. In this chapter, we have shown that results in the other two research chapters support a tracking mechanism. We have provided such a data-led mechanism to track regime changes dynamically. This is a practical method, as it uses data up to the present to monitor the likelihood of the market entering a volatile regime.

The proposed approach used TMV and T values observed in the two regimes in the past to establish a Naïve Bayes classifier. For each pair of (TMV, T) values observed in the current market, the Bayes classifier calculated two probabilities: one for the market being in Regime 1 (the "normal regime" in Chapter 4) and one for the market being in Regime 2 (the "abnormal regime" in terms of volatility). These two probabilities are used to decide which regime the market is in. Two classification rules were examined: a Simple Rule and a Stricter Rule. Combined with the Bayes classifier, the tracking systems are called B-Simple and B-Strict, respectively.

In the experiment, the data of Dow Jones, FTSE 100 and S&P 500 index from 2007 to 2009 were used to build the NBC. The model was then used to track each index from 2010 to 2012. By using the method presented in Chapter 3, we concluded, with the benefit of hindsight, two spells of Regime 2 in the test period. Both B-Simple and B-Strict managed to pick up both spells. In our view, these results are very positive. The tracking signals could be useful to market participants. This work potentially lays the foundation for a financial early warning system, warning market participants of market instability, which influence the outcome of local, national and international financial markets.

However, this chapter is a proof of concept, and thus part of a beginning of the research on this topic. It uses a Naïve Bayes classifier and two very simple classification rules for its proof. No doubt more experiments will need to be done and more advanced methods could be developed in the future to improve the reliability and usability of the tracking in future research.

CHAPTER 6

Algorithmic Trading Based on Regime Change Tracking

6.1 OVERVIEW

I N Chapter 5, we presented our method to track regime changes in financial markets. The tracking signals produced by this method suggest whether the market is shifting from one regime to another or remaining in the present regime. In this chapter, we examine the usefulness of this tracking information for trading. Could this information help us apply different trading strategies under different regimes? Could the regime tracking information generated by our method in Chapter 5 be used as early warnings, using one of our specific trading algorithms? Could a trading algorithm benefit from such warnings to better understand the market and capitalise on the position? Would such signals help an algorithm to reduce maximum drawdown?

In order to answer the above questions, we designed two simple trading algorithms, which make use of regime tracking information generated by the method presented in Chapter 5. By comparing their performance with the simple contrarian algorithm empirically, we shall examine the impact of the regime tracking information discovered using these algorithms.

This chapter is structured as follows: Section 6.1 introduces the purpose and contributions of this chapter. Section 6.2 describes the designed trading algorithms: JC1 and JC2. Section 6.3 explains the experimental set up. Experiment results are presented in Section 6.4. These results are interpreted and discussed in Section 6.5. Section 6.6 concludes this chapter.

6.2 METHODOLOGY

In the previous chapters, we have for the first time demonstrated how to detect regime changes from historical data, using Directional Change (Chapter 3), to classify market regimes (Chapter 4), and how to track the market to probabilistically recognize the regime at the moment of tracking (Chapter 5). In this chapter, we will further develop our position, in order to examine whether our regime detection has a practical impact on algorithmic trading[1].

To examine the effect of regime tracking on trading, two trading algorithms are designed: JC1 and JC2. These are DC-based trading algorithms supported by regime tracking information produced by the method proposed in Chapter 5. Both of these trading algorithms use regime tracking information to close positions; the aim of doing so is to reduce the maximum drawdown. JC1 would adopt different strategies in normal and abnormal regimes (as defined in Chapter 4), whereas JC1 only trades under normal regimes. JC1 and JC2 are compared to a simple contrarian algorithm, CT1, which is not supported by any regime tracking information. Table 6.1 summarises the trading algorithms used in this chapter. Details will be elaborated in the sections that follow.

6.2.1 Regime Tracking Information

In Chapter 3, we showed that regime change is detected in hindsight. In Chapter 5, we proposed a method for tracking the market with the aim to determine the current market regime. To recapitulate, the tracking mechanism works as follows: first, regime changes are detected in the historical data. This information will then be used for calculating the likely regime change of the given data set. Second, we need to extract information up to the current point, namely readings of the two DC

---

[1]Algorithmic trading is where a computer program will follow an algorithm in order to trade, which, in theory is meant to produce profits at a frequency and speed that is not possible for a human trader, and is growing in importance, in the 24 hour, global financial system, and by 2007, 60% of orders at the London Stock Exchange were carried out by algorithmic traders. (*The Economist*, June, 2019)

Table 6.1: Summary of algorithms used (DCC = DC Confirmation, RCD = Regime Change Detected by the method presented in Chapter 5).

Algorithms		JC1	JC2	CT1
Under **Normal** Regime	Open	Open **contrarian** position when $|TMV|$ reaches 2	Open **contrarian** position when $|TMV|$ reaches 2	Open **contrarian** position when $|TMV|$ reaches 2
	Close	Close at next DCC or **RCD**	Close at next DCC or **RCD**	Close at next DCC
Under **Abnormal** Regime	Open	Open **trend following** position when $|TMV|$ reaches 2	(No trades)	Same as in Normal Regime
	Close	Close at next DCC or **RCD**		

indicators, TMV and T, in the current trend. Lastly, a naïve Bayes model is applied to calculate the likelihood of the current regime, based on the information of regime changes that is learnt from the historical data.

6.2.2   Trading Algorithm JC1

Trading algorithm JC1 is built from both the regime change tracking signals and DC. To take advantage of the regime information, it attempts to apply different strategies under different regimes.

Glattfelder et al. [27] showed that in the foreign exchange market, on average, the market changes direction at $TMV = 2$. Golub et al. [28] presented a trading algorithm, which they named the Alpha Engine, a contrarian algorithm based on this observation. As a contrarian algorithm, it trades against the prevailing market trends. One of the problems observed in the Alpha Engine was that, occasionally, it suffers from heavy drawdown. The Alpha Engine is profitable in most trades. However, heavy drawdowns wipe out the cumulated profits.

Built into JC1 are two distinct features which make use of regime tracking information:

1. When regime change is detected, JC1 closes its positions. The aim of doing so is to avoid big drawdowns (which is precisely the problem faced by the Alpha Engine).

2. When the market is in the normal regime, JC1 trades as a contrarian. Under the abnormal regime, JC1 trades as a trend-follower. This is an attempt to use different trading strategies for different markets.

The opening rules are: when absolute value of TMV reaches 2, open a contrarian position. Since TMV measures the price change from one extreme point to the next extreme point, a positive TMV indicates an upward trend and a negative TMV indicates a downward trend. Therefore, if the trend is going up, JC1 opens a short position at $TMV = 2$. If the trend is going down, JC1 opens a long position at $TMV = -2$.

Two closing rules are designed: first, close the position at the next DC Confirmation (DCC) point. Secondly, close any open position when regime change is concluded. Following is a summary of the rules under normal markets:

JC1 under <u>Normal</u> Regime:

Rule 1: In an uptrend, when $TMV \geqslant 2$, open a short position.

Rule 2: In a downtrend, when $TMV \leqslant -2$, open a long position.

Rule 3: When the next DCC point is confirmed, close the current position.

Rule 4: When regime change is concluded, close the current position.

If the market is under an abnormal regime, a trend-following trading strategy will be applied. Following are the rules used under abnormal markets:

JC1 under <u>Abnormal</u> Regime:

Rule 1a: In an uptrend, when $TMV \geqslant 2$, open a long position.

Rule 2a: In a downtrend, when $TMV \leqslant -2$, open a short position.

Rule 3a: When the next DCC point is confirmed, close the current position.

Rule 4a: When regime change is concluded, close the current position.

There are a few rationales behind the above algorithm. For example, a contrarian trading strategy is applied in the normal regime. This is because mean reversion is observed in the normal market regime. Mean reversion is a theory applied in finance, which suggests that the asset price will revert to its mean or average level in the long run. It is also observed under DC [27]. That is why a contrarian algorithm normally works.

On the other hand, in the abnormal regimes, a trend-following strategy is implemented. This strategy is applied because an abnormal market regime in this research is measured by a rapid change of prices (large R). When the market is in an abnormal regime, margin calls become more likely. Margin calls tend to drive the trend further forward. That is why a trend-following algorithm is likely to work.

6.2.3   Trading Algorithm JC2

Trading algorithm JC2 uses the same trading rules as JC1, except that it only trades under the normal regime. It closes its positions as soon as the tracking concludes that the market has entered an abnormal regime. JC2 will not trade again until the market returns to the normal regime. In other words, JC2 holds no positions under the abnormal regime. Following are the trading rules of JC2:

JC2 under <u>Normal</u> Regime:

Rule 1: In an uptrend, when $TMV \geqslant 2$, open a short position.

Rule 2: In a downtrend, when $TMV \leqslant -2$, open a long position.

Rule 3: When regime change is concluded, close the current position.

No Trades under <u>Abnormal</u> Regime.

6.2.4   Control Algorithm CT1

Control algorithm uses the same trading rules as algorithm JC2, except that it does not use regime tracking information. It is used as a benchmark to evaluate algorithm JC2, to measure the impact of the tracking information. Following are the trading rules of CT1:

CT1:

Rule 1: In an uptrend, when $TMV \geqslant 2$, open a short position.

Rule 2: In a downtrend, when $TMV \leqslant -2$, open a long position.

Rule 3: When the next DCC point is confirmed, close the current position.

6.3 EXPERIMENTAL SETUP

This section introduces an experimental setup to evaluate the trading algorithm. This includes the data used, the parameters of the experiment and money management by the trading algorithms.

6.3.1 Data

In this experiment, three sets of stock indices are used to test the proposed trading algorithms. The chosen stock indices are:

- Dow Jones Industrial Average (DJIA),

- FTSE 100, and

- S&P 500.

For each index, the daily closing price is recorded from 2 January 2007 to 31 December 2012. The chosen data set is the same as that used in Chapter 5. This allows to show that the impact of regime tracking results in Chapter 5 on algorithmic trading. As discussed in Section 6.2, trading algorithms JC1 and JC2 will make use of the regime tracking results of Chapter 5.

The data set is separated into two parts. The first part is used for learning the characteristics of abnormal and abnormal regimes (as described in Chapter 4). The second part is for regime tracking (using the naïve Bayes model described in Chapter 5). Tracking information is then used by trading algorithms, JC1, and JC2. Table 6.2 shows the time ranges of the training and tracking data sets.

6.3.2 Experimental Parameters

To implement the designed algorithm for investment, a few parameters need to be decided. The first one is the threshold that is used to measure DC trends in the training periods of the data. It is called *regime*

Table 6.2: Time periods of training and tracking data set.

Data Set	Time Periods	
	Training Periods	**Tracking Periods**
DJIA	03/01/2007–31/12/2009	01/01/2010–28/12/2012
FTSE 100	03/01/2007–31/12/2009	01/01/2010–28/12/2012
S&P 500	03/01/2007–31/12/2009	01/01/2010–28/12/2012

tracking threshold. The resulted DC trends are used to establish a naïve Bayes model for regime tracking.

JC1, JC2 and CT1 are all DC-based trading algorithms. To apply these algorithms, we need to decide on the DC threshold, which we call the *trading threshold.* This is our second parameter.

The final parameter is the regime tracking rule (see Chapter 5 for details). Two rules were introduced in Chapter 5: B-Simple and B-Strict.

With the input arguments, the designed algorithms could be defined as:

$$JC1(\theta, \alpha, \beta), JC2(\theta, \alpha, \beta), CT1(\theta, \alpha, \beta), \qquad (6.1)$$

where θ is the regime tracking threshold, α is the trading threshold and β is the regime tracking rule.

In our experiments, the regime tracking threshold θ is set to 0.003. To examine the effect of trading threshold on the performance of the algorithm, three different trading thresholds are used: α takes a value in $\{0.03, 0.006, 0.009\}$. As for regime tracking, β is set to the rule *B-Simple.*

6.3.3 Money Management

We have defined above when JC1, JC2 and CT1 open and close positions in response to DC and Regime Change (RC) conditions. We need to decide how much of the capital to trade under these conditions.

We adopt a simple strategy for all the algorithms that we test: (1) We assume that the trading algorithm starts with a fixed amount of money, M. (2) When an algorithm opens a long position, it trades with all its wealth. That means if the index price is at P, then the algorithm will buy M divided by P shares of the index. Here we assume, for simplicity, that one can hold any fraction of the index. (3) When an algorithm opens a short position, it will also short-sell M divided by P shares of the index.

We adopt these simple rules because money management is not the main research topic in this book. More importantly, these simple rules should not have impact on the relative performance of the trading algorithms tested.

6.4 EXPERIMENT RESULTS

It this section, evidence is provided to evaluate the three algorithms designed: JC1, JC2 and CT1.

The next question is how to measure the performance of an algorithm. First, the final wealth of the investment using each algorithm is compared. This is to show whether the algorithm is able to generate a profit.

A second and arguably more important performance indicator is the maximum drawdown. It measures the biggest loss in all the trades by an algorithm. It is important because we hope that the tracking information is useful for raising early alarms. If these early alarms are useful, we should expect them to reduce the maximum drawdown of JC1 and JC2.

For completeness, we shall also report the number of trades. This is mainly for verifying that the final wealth and maximum drawdown are based on a sufficient number of trades.

6.4.1 Number of Trades

First, we look at the number of trades made by the algorithms JC1, JC2 and CT1. This is to ensure that the results are based on enough number of trades. If results are based on too few trades, they could be biased over one of two lucky or unlucky trades.

Table 6.3, Table 6.4 and Table 6.5 show the number of trades that JC1, CT1 and JC2 made using trading thresholds 0.03, 0.006 and 0.009, respectively. As expected, the bigger the trading thresholds, the fewer trends one sees in a market period. For example, under trading threshold 0.03, which is the biggest of the three thresholds used, JC1 made 26 trades in DJIA, CT1 made 25 trades and JC2 made 21 trades (see Table 6.3).

We concluded that there were a sufficient number of trades to make the results statistically acceptable. Under trading thresholds 0.006 and

0.009, number of trades were in the 60 to 90 ranges. This gives us confidence that the results are not biased by a few extremely lucky or unlucky trades.

Table 6.3: Number of trades with trading threshold 0.03.

Data Set	Number of Trades		
	JC1	CT1	JC2
DJIA	26	25	21
FTSE 100	28	27	22
S&P 500	29	29	20

Table 6.4: Number of trades with trading threshold 0.006.

Data Set	Number of Trades		
	JC1	CT1	JC2
DJIA	73	73	70
FTSE 100	82	82	81
S&P 500	68	68	68

Table 6.5: Number of trades with trading threshold 0.009.

Data Set	Number of Trades		
	JC1	CT1	JC2
DJIA	66	66	66
FTSE 100	72	72	71
S&P 500	70	70	69

6.4.2 Final Wealth

In this section, we compare the final wealth of the three trading algorithms tested. To recapitulate, JC1 and JC2 are trading algorithms that use the regime tracking information. CT1 is the control algorithm which operates on the same trading rules as JC1, except that it is not using regime tracking results. We report the performance of the algorithms under different trading thresholds. Table 6.6 shows final wealth of the algorithms that are using a trading threshold of 0.03; the most favourable results among the algorithms are highlighted. Results in Table 6.6 show that the final wealth of JC1 and JC2 are both inferior to that of CT1. For DJIA, CT1 gained a final wealth of 131% (i.e., a gain of 31%), compared to 113% in JC1 and 121% in JC2. Similar results are obtained in FTSE and GSPC.

Similar results are observed under trading thresholds 0.006 (see Table 6.7) and 0.009 (see Table 6.8). The only exception is in FTSE 100 under trading threshold of 0.006 (Table 6.7, second to last row). There, the final wealth of CT1 was 97% (i.e., a loss of 3%), but JC1 and JC2 had a final wealth of 100% and 99%, respectively.

Table 6.6: Final wealth with trading threshold 0.03.

Data Set	Final Wealth		
	JC1	CT1	JC2
DJIA	113%	131%	121%
FTSE 100	106%	128%	109%
S&P 500	83%	134%	102%

Table 6.7: Final wealth with trading threshold 0.006.

Data Set	Final Wealth		
	JC1	CT1	JC2
DJIA	87%	101%	93%
FTSE 100	100%	97%	99%
S&P 500	80%	82%	80%

Table 6.8: Final wealth with trading threshold 0.009.

Data Set	Final Wealth		
	JC1	CT1	JC2
DJIA	87%	92%	87%
FTSE 100	86%	94%	86%
S&P 500	82%	97%	84%

6.4.3 Maximum Drawdown

As the primary function of tracking information is to raise early alarms, the maximum drawdown is our key performance indicator. It measures the effectiveness of the early alarms.

The maximum drawdown of JC1, CT1, and JC2, under different thresholds is listed in Table 6.9, Table 6.10 and Table 6.11. Results show that the maximum drawdown of JC1 and JC2 is both smaller than that of CT1 in all three markets. For example, under trading threshold 0.003 (Table 6.9), the maximum drawdown of JC1 and JC2 is 5% for DJIA, which is 1% smaller than the 6% suffered by CT1. Under trading threshold 0.009 (Table 6.11), the maximum drawdown of both JC1 and JC2 is 7% for GSPC, which is 3% better than the maximum drawdown of CT1, which is 10%.

These results consistently prove that the tracking information is useful as an effective early alarm system for trading.

Table 6.9: Maximum drawdown 0.03.

Data Set	Final Wealth		
	JC1	CT1	JC2
DJIA	-5%	-6%	-5%
FTSE 100	-4%	-5%	-4%
S&P 500	-5%	-8%	-6%

Table 6.10: Maximum drawdown 0.006.

Data Set	Final Wealth		
	JC1	CT1	JC2
DJIA	-9%	-10%	-9%
FTSE 100	-10%	-11%	-9%
S&P 500	-8%	-11%	-8%

Table 6.11: Maximum drawdown 0.09.

Data Set	Final Wealth		
	JC1	CT1	JC2
DJIA	-6%	-7%	-6%
FTSE 100	-8%	-10%	-8%
S&P 500	-7%	-10%	-7%

6.5 DISCUSSIONS

6.5.1 The Primary Goals Are Achieved

The above results support the following claims:

1. Regime position information helps to reduce maximum draw-down: Results show that closing a position when the regime

changes in the market reduces maximum drawdown. In other words, closing one's position when the market changes its regime is an effective stop-loss strategy.

2. The quality of our regime tracking is good enough to support JC1 and JC2: For JC1 and JC2 to work, the quality of the regime information produced by our method in Chapter 5 must be reasonably reliable. If this is not the case, JC1 and JC2 will not benefit from such information.

6.5.2 Future Work: Regime Tracking for Better Trading Algorithms

The difference between JC1 and JC2, is that the former trades in abnormal regimes, but the latter does not. JC1 implements a naïve strategy in trading under abnormal regimes. The performance of JC2 is generally better than that of JC1. This suggests that the strategy that JC1 uses under abnormal regimes is too primitive.

JC1 and JC2 are primitive trading algorithms. They are useful for proving our point, which is the usefulness of regime tracking information. They are both inferior to the control algorithm CT1 in profitability. We conjecture that the regime tracking information is effective for reducing maximum drawdown for more complicated algorithms. This is left for future research.

One possibility is to add regime tracking information to the Alpha Engine [28]. The Alpha Engine experience shows that a DC-based contrarian trading strategy in general accumulates profits over trades but suffers from big drawdowns. If we could reduce maximum drawdowns, we could improve the performance of the Alpha Engine. This is also left for future research.

6.6 CONCLUSIONS

In this chapter, we examine the usefulness of regime tracking information produced in Chapter 5 on trading. For that purpose, we have designed an algorithm CT1, which is a simple contrarian trading algorithm. We have designed two variations of JC1 and JC2, which use regime tracking information produced by the method in Chapter 5 in CT1. JC2 extends CT1 by using regime change information to close positions; besides, JC2 ceases to trade under abnormal regime. JC1 extends JC2 by trading as a trend-following strategy under abnormal regime; it attempts to adopt different trading strategies under different regimes.

We tested the three algorithms in different assets using different trading thresholds. Results demonstrated consistently that regime tracking information helped JC1 and JC2 reduce their maximum drawdown. It also proved that the regime information produced by the method in Chapter 5 is reasonably accurate.

It is worth noting that JC1 and JC2 are very naïve trading strategies. Therefore, the low returns of JC1 and JC2 compared to the control algorithm CT1 should not deter researchers from using regime tracking information to improve profitability of more advanced algorithms, such as the Alpha Machine [28]. Neither should the results of JC1 deter researchers from designing different trading strategies under different regimes. With proven success in reducing maximum drawdown, regime tracking information is valuable to algorithmic trading research.

CHAPTER 7

Conclusions

T HIS chapter provides a brief overall summary of the book. It indicates the ideas explored, the research carried out, and what has been the sequence of our work to promote the themes of our research. Also, there is consideration given to what is the likely future areas for further research, leading on from our current work.

This chapter is organised as follows: Section 7.1 provides a brief summary of the presented work in this book. The contributions of this book are summarised in Section 7.2. The likely directions for further research are provided in Section 7.3.

7.1   SUMMARY OF WORK DONE

This book, as is indicated by its title, is concerned with establishing effective recognition of the occurrence of regime change in financial markets. During the past two decades, financial markets have experienced a rapid change and expansion, with a huge growth in market activity, and the computerization of market activity and trading. The development and growth of artificial intelligence also looks likely to make a significant and unpredictable impact on the operation of world-wide financial markets in the future. The continuing moves towards capital market liberalization also will continue this expansion around the world with the continuing growth of global financial markets. There is thus a move towards what the critic Paul Virilio called *deterritorialisation* [50], or a new *telemetrical becoming*, with a possible projected future of unleashed global markets and friction-free capitalism. Thus, new methods and techniques are increasingly needed to be able to effectively monitor, track and study data from these new, changing financial markets, markets that have also increasingly relied on trends of market efficiency.

The research that we have undertaken in this book provides a new perspective to recognise and understand significant changes in financial markets, which are defined as regime change in this book. In Chapter 1, we discussed the concept of regime changes, and the need for new methods to recognise and analyse them in financial markets. This discussion led on to the research objectives of this book.

The current research available on regime change was outlined in Chapter 2. The literature survey indicated that most of the existing regime change detection methods were established based on time series analysis. Although time series is currently the most used technique for the analysis of market behaviour, there are drawbacks associated with time series. For example, data in time series is recorded at fixed time intervals, which runs the risk of missing a significant or important market shift, as markets can now be tracked with data extracted from 24-hour high-frequency trading, such as in the foreign exchange market.

Therefore, to develop a new method to recognise regime changes in financial markets, we introduced Directional Change (DC) as a new way of providing an effective extraction of market information and analysis of financial data. In contrast to time series, DC, which is a data-driven approach, is able to recognise regime change movement when it occurs, as DC samples the extreme points of the movement of the market when they occur. It is therefore able to record market movement and fluctuations which might otherwise be missed by time series. In our view, DC is an effective and new way to interpret the establishment of different regimes through effective tracking of the dynamics of the market and its price movements.

Apart from DC, the relevant machine learning techniques which we adapted in this book were also outlined in Chapter 2. For instance, in the first research (Chapter 3), the Hidden Markov model (HMM) was combined with DC to discover regime changes. And in the third research chapter (Chapter 5), the Naïve Bayes classifier was applied to track market changes, from DC market data.

However, given our book concept about regime change and DC, there was a need for it to be tested, in order to explore how to effectively use DC in data analysis, to recognise regime changes in financial markets. In the first research study, which was presented in Chapter 3, we proposed a new approach to detect regime change in financial markets. This approach was based on the framework of DC, which was different from the conventional time series approach. Under our chosen DC framework, we used a variable DC indicator, DC Return, to summarise the fluctuation of the financial data. The DC indicator was compared with a time series variable, that of realised volatility, in regime change detection.

To evaluate the efficiency of using DC to recognise regime changes, we used the observed variables from both DC data and time series, into an HMM. This combination of machine learning techniques resulted in regime change being clearly recognised. This approach was then examined using a chosen period of time when the market was likely to be experiencing a regime change. The financial data was taken from a period of market uncertainty and fluctuation, over the period of two months, spanning the UK's referendum vote over whether to leave the European Union, or Brexit, from the period 23 May 2016 to 22 July 2016.

The results indicated that both DC and time series were able to achieve regime change recognition. The detected regime changes from both DC data and time series corresponded to the major market event, the period of the Brexit referendum. Moreover, we found that the DC approach was able to detect regime change not recorded under time series. Therefore, according to our research, it is the use of the two techniques together, that of time series and DC, to establish regime change, that would enable the researcher to examine the data more fully, to achieve a fuller picture and a clear recognition of regime change in financial markets.

In addition, our research indicated that the results of the regime changes which were detected under DC and time series could be broken down into two clearly definable regimes: Regime 1, with low volatility and Regime 2, with high volatility.

Based on the findings in Chapter 3, we went on to study regime change under the framework of DC. In the second part of our research, in Chapter 4, we examined the occurrence of the market regimes in greater detail, and were able to categorise market regimes into "normal market regimes" and "abnormal market regimes".

Thus, using our development of DC and the HMM together, we attempted to classify the two types of market regimes with historical data from 10 financial markets. The results demonstrated that normal regimes across different financial markets shared similar statistical characteristics. In addition, by observing the DC indicators in a designed two-dimensional indicator space, we were able to distinguish normal from abnormal regimes, so that it was possible to clearly establish what regime a market currently inhabited.

In our view, our research also shows the importance of significant external events affecting the fluctuations of the financial markets. According to our research, the abnormal regime (more volatile market periods) was more likely to have been triggered by a significant external event, such as the oil crash of 2014–2016, or the global financial crisis of 2007–2008, but then the market always returned to and stayed in normal regimes (less volatile market periods) afterwards.

Our research also indicated that it is possible to tell whether a market is in a normal regime by observing the DC indicators in the market. This suggested that the DC indicators could potentially be used to track the market, to see whether regime change transition between normal and abnormal regimes is occurring. This would allow for real time tracking of financial markets, with implications for both financial trading and financial market tracking.

Our third research chapter, Chapter 5, went on to further examine this point, to widen the scope of the recognition of regime change, by using the DC indicators to track regime change dynamically. Based on the findings in Chapter 3 and Chapter 4, in this research chapter we proposed a new method to track the transition of regime changes.

This is a practical method which allows us to track regime changes up to the present. We observed the DC indicators of the two regimes (Regime 1 or 2) from the past financial data. A Bayesian probability model was introduced to analyse the data generated from the DC indicators. Then, given the financial data up to the present, the Bayesian model was able to uncover the probabilities and likelihoods of which regime the market is in.

In the empirical study, we used the data from the Dow Jones, FTSE 100 and S&P 500 index from 2007 to 2010, to track regime changes of the data of the S&P 500 index from 2010 to 2012. The results show that the proposed method is capable of picking up the signals of regime changes. Therefore, we can conclude that by observing the information from the past financial data under DC, we are able to make an assumption in real time as to what regime the market is in.

In our fourth research chapter, Chapter 6, we demonstrated that the information of regime tracking can be applied to establish trading algorithms. We proposed two trading algorithms which make use of the regime tracking signals. In the empirical study, these two algorithms are compared with the control algorithm without using the tracking signals. Results suggest that regime tracking information helped reduce their maximum drawdown. It means by adopting different strategies under different regimes, investors can minimize their losses in their investment.

Thus, our four linked areas of DC research provided a new approach to measuring the market dynamics of regime change, indicating that, in our view, DC analysis is an effective tool for use by financial market researchers, for financial market analysis, as well as those involved in oversight of the financial market.

Finally, it is worth noting that both regime change detection (Chapters 3 and 4) and tracking (Chapter 5) are data driven. The data indicates to us whether the market is in the normal or abnormal regime. No forecasting is attempted. It is up to users to interpret what are the results.

7.2 TAKE-HOME MESSAGES

The research work explored in this book provides a new way to understand and measure the dynamic of financial markets in terms of regime changes. Combining different machine learning techniques with a data-driven method, that of Directional Change, new methods are provided to detect regime changes in the financial market, to categorise different market regimes and to dynamically track the transition of regime changes from the information observed up to the present. The main contributions of this book are:

1. The use of Directional Change (DC) variable Return (R) in a machine learning model (namely, HMM) proposed in Chapter 3 is the first attempt to detect regime change under the DC framework. Tested on the foreign exchange market, the regime changes detected by the proposed method and their timings are consistent with political developments over the Brexit referendum in the UK in June 2016.

2. We have shown in Chapter 3 that using DC and time series together gave us more insight into the occurrence and timing of regime changes, rather than using DC or time series alone. To be precise, while regime changes detected by the DC method proposed in Chapter 3 agreed with regime changes detected under time series most of the time, the results are not identical. For example, DC detected a short spell of regime change (14/07/2016

07:03:12 to 07:05:01, see Table 3.1) which was not detected under time series.

3. This is the first attempt to establish what are the statistical properties of normal and abnormal regimes in terms of their positions in the DC indicators space (Chapter 4). Through the observation of regimes detected in ten different markets at different times using different thresholds, we discovered that normal and abnormal regimes (which represent regimes before and after significant events took place) are clearly separable in the normalised TMV and T indicator space.

4. As a proof of concept, we have proposed (in Chapter 5) a method to track the market using the statistical properties established in Chapter 4. By feeding the TMV and T observed in the current trend into a Naïve Bayes classifier, we can independently compute the probabilities of the current market being in the normal or in the abnormal regimes. By using a simple rule, we can combine these probabilities to conjecture whether the current market is in the normal or abnormal regime. Preliminary results suggest that the proposed method managed to detect regime change signals accurately and promptly.

5. In Chapter 6, we examined the usefulness of the regime tracking information. Two trading algorithms are proposed which make use of the regime tracking signals that are presented in Chapter 5. The results show that the regime tracking signals help to reduce maximum drawdown in investment.

To summarise, this book has pioneered a method for regime change detection under the DC framework. It showed that normal and abnormal regimes can be characterised using two DC indicators, TMV and T. Such characteristics once established could be used for market tracking, which potentially lays the foundation of building practical financial early warning systems.

7.3 FUTURE RESEARCH

This book has used DC to attempt to successfully understand the financial market more fully, in the area of regime change, which has proved sensitive to both external significant events as well as those of market fluctuations. Given that a new method is provided to detect and measure regime changes in financial markets, there is a wide range of opportunities to carry out more research on regime changes under DC. We have shown in this book that DC provides new perspectives to market analysis. Therefore, DC is a framework that financial data scientists should not ignore.

7.3.1 Research Directions

In Chapter 3, a new method is proposed to detect regime changes in financial markets. With this method, the HMM is applied to recognise regime changes from the observation of DC. However, only two types of market regimes are defined in this research: normal regime with lower volatility (which is reflected by smaller R) and abnormal regime with high volatility. Since the market obviously fluctuates during extreme events, it is worth to discover and define more likely market regimes, based on different market conditions.

Besides, in this research, a significant market event is attached to every selected data set. As a result, a significant event is attached to every detected market regime. This is because we want to see if the detected regime changes are related to some significant market events. Also, this allows us to relate the timing of the regime changes to the significant events. However, it is possible that a regime change happens in the market without being caused by any event that we are aware of. This is because extreme events could cause changes in volatility, but volatility change does not necessarily cause regime changes. Therefore, another interesting research direction would be to investigate regime changes in a long period of time with the proposed method, and to find out if regime changes would be detected without being caused by significant market events.

Using the proposed method, ten financial assets are investigated in Chapter 4. The detected market regimes are then plotted into a two-dimensional DC indicator space: the T-TMV space. The results show that the positions of normal and abnormal regimes are clearly separable from each other in the T-TMV space. This allows us to classify normal and abnormal regimes according to their positions in the indicator space.

Equipped with characteristics of the normal and abnormal regimes, one promising research path is to go forward to measure the distance between the positions of normal and abnormal regimes in the indicator space. This would allow us to measure the statistical differences between two regimes. Moreover, one could apply some machine learning models, such as the support vector machines (SVMs) to find a clear gap between two categories. It may lead to the discovery of the boundary between normal and abnormal regimes.

The characteristics of the normal and abnormal regimes are applied for market tracking in Chapter 5. As a proof of concept, we proposed a market tracking method to compute the probability of the current market being in normal and abnormal regime.

In Chapter 6, we have demonstrated how predicted regime signals could help trading. We acknowledge that the predictions are not always perfect, and more can be done. Trading should benefit from better predictions. For example, we observe that there are too many Regime 2 signals generated by B-Simple, and very few by B-Strict. One could attempt to improve the accuracy of a regime tracking system by, for example, taking the average of the signals. Besides, one could also attempt to look for a confirmatory signal following the initial signal. These are promising research areas forward.

Aside from trading with regime change signals, another research path would be to establish an early warning system based on the tracking signals of regime changes. The proposed market tracking method manage to monitor the transition of market regimes up to the present. This could lead to the establishment of a practical financial early warning system, which could raise the alarm when the transition of market regimes is detected. Such research could be useful for market makers and regulators to monitor the financial market.

Finally, since only one threshold was used to sample data in the proposed market tracking method, multiple thresholds could also be applied to track the market.

A Formal Definition of Directional Change

T HIS appendix gives a formal definition of Directional Change. As the definitions are mutually recursive, some terms are used before they are well defined. Directional Change takes an event-based view of the market. This appendix also relates this event-based view to the point-based view, which may be more familiar to some readers.

DEFINITIONS OF DIRECTIONAL CHANGE EVENTS

At any time, the market is either in a **Downward Run** or an **Upward Run**. A Downward Run comprises a **Downturn Event** and a subsequent **Downward Overshoot Event**. An Upward Run comprises an **Upturn Event** followed by a subsequent **Upward Overshoot Event**.

In a Downward Run, a **Last Low** is constantly updated to the minimum of (a) the current price and (b) the Last Low. In an Upward Run, a **Last High** is constantly updated to the maximum of (a) the current price and (b) the Last High.

Given a **Threshold** θ (a percentage), a Downward Run is confirmed to have ended when a price P is found to be higher than the Last Low by θ. The event of price change from the Last Low to P is called the **Upward Directional Change Event**. The Last Low (which is now confirmed to be a **Trough**) terminates the preceding Downward Run and starts the next Upward Run. P is called the **Upward DC Confirmation Point** for the Upward Run.

Given a Threshold θ, an Upward Run is confirmed to have ended when a price P' is found to be lower than the Last High by θ. The event of the price change from the Last High to P' is called the **Downward Directional Change Event**. The Last High (which is now confirmed to be a **Peak**) terminates the preceding Upward Run and starts the next Downward Run. P' is called the **Downward DC Confirmation Point** for the Down Run.

The event of price change from the Downward DC Confirmation point to the Trough in a Downward Run is called the **Downward Overshoot Event**. The Event of price change from the Upward DC Confirmation point to the Peak in an Upward Run is called the **Upward Overshoot Event**.

The above definitions are mutual recursive. Operationally, before one knows whether the market is in an Upward Run or Downward Run, one sets both the Last High and Last Low to the price at the beginning of the sequence.

Time is therefore defined by cycles of four events, as shown in Figure A.1.

... $\rightarrow$ Downward Directional Change Event $\rightarrow$
Downward Overshoot Event $\rightarrow$
Upward Directional Change Event $\rightarrow$
Upward Overshoot Event $\rightarrow$
Downward Directional Change Event $\rightarrow$ ...

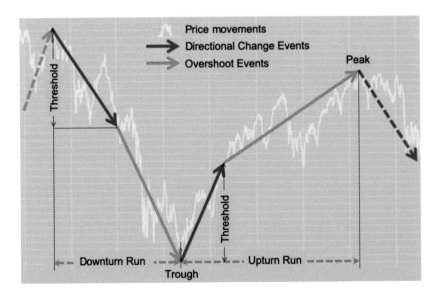

FIGURE A.1: Examples of Directional Change and Overshoot Events.

TIME ONTOLOGY

What is time exactly? The most studied ontologies were mainly based on **point**, **intervals** and **events** [49]. Most people in finance are familiar with a point-based analysis. For example, people talk about the price or a commodity at a certain time (e.g., 1:23pm) on a certain day. Directional change research adopts the event ontology. Under this ontology, time is defined by events (one could say that when no events takes place, there is no notion of time).

A directional change event is a primary object in an event-based system. Intervals and points are secondary objects.

In physical time, which is popularly seen in a point-based system, an interval is a continuous set of points. In a point-based system, a Downward DC Event can be seen as a process that occupies an interval. One could define the starting point of a Downturn Event as a **Downturn Point** and the end of a Downward DC Event a **Downturn Confirmation Point**. The Downturn Point is the point at which the price last peaked. The Downturn Confirmation Point is the point at which the price has dropped by the threshold (percentage) from the Downturn Point. Similarly, one can define the start and end points of an Upward Directional Change Event as **Upturn Point** and **Upturn Confirmation Point**.

Under this stipulation, the **Downward DC Event Interval (DEI)** is the set of all points between the Downturn Point and the Downturn Confirmation Point. (Here one can debate whether the interval should or should not include the Downturn Confirmation Point; we adopt the latter in our formal definition below.) The **Upward DC Event Interval (UEI)** is the set of all points between the Upturn Point and the Upturn Confirmation Point. Formally, they are defined as follows:

$$DEI =_{def} \{t|\text{Downturn Point} \leq t < \text{Downturn Confirmation Point}\}$$
$$UEI =_{def} \{t|\text{Upturn Point} \leq t < \text{Upturn Confirmation Point}\}$$

$$(A.1)$$

The Downward Overshoot Event is a process that occupies an interval, which we refer to as the **Downward Overshoot Interval (DOI)**, which is the set of all points between the previous Downturn Confirmation Point and the next Upturn Point. Similarly, an **Upward Overshoot Interval (UOI)** is the set of all points between the previous Upturn Confirmation Point and the next Downturn Point:

$$DOI =_{def} \{t | \text{Previous Downturn Confirmation Point}$$
$$\leq t < \text{Next Upturn Point}\}$$
$$UOI =_{def} \{t | \text{Previous Upturn Confirmation Point}$$
$$\leq t < \text{Next Downturn Point}\} \qquad (A.2)$$

The relationship between our event-based system and the point-based system is shown in Figure A.2. For a full account of time ontology, and relationship between different time systems, readers are referred to [49].

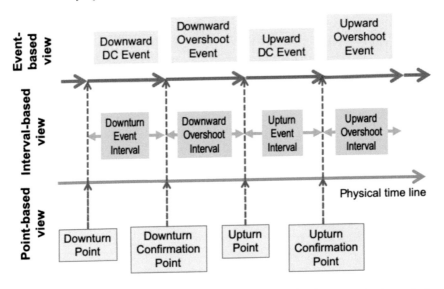

FIGURE A.2: Summary of terminology and relating events to points.

EX-ANTE AND POST-ANTE VIEWS UNDER DIFFERENT TIME SYSTEMS

It is worth noting that in the point-based system, at the Downturn Point, we do not know that a Downturn Event has started. We would only know that a Downward DC Event has happened at the Downward DC Confirmation Point. Similarly, we only know that an Upturn Events has happened at the Upward DC Confirmation Point.

According to our definition, Overshooting Events are events in between Directional Change Events. For that reason, as soon as a Downturn Event is confirmed, we know that a Downward Overshoot Event has started. However, we will not know when it ends until the next Upward DC Event is confirmed. This means an Upturn Confirmation Point does not only confirm an Upward DC Event, it also confirms the end the last Upturn Point (trough), which is the end of the last Downturn Overshoot Event. The ex-ante and post-ante views are summarised in Table A.1.

Table A.1: Summary of different views for different events (views on Upturn and Upturn Overshoot Events are similar and omitted here).

Events	Points	Post-Ante Views	Ex-Ante Confirmation Views
Downturn Event	Start	Downturn Point (peak)	Downward DC Confirmation Point
	End	Downward DC Confirmation Point	Downward DC Confirmation Point
Downturn Overshoot Event	Start	Downward DC Confirmation Point	Last Downward DC Confirmation Point
	End	Next Upturn Point (trough)	Next Upward DC Confirmation Point

Extended Results of Chapter 3

In this appendix, we provided the extend results of the experiment that were presented in Chapter 3. Table B.1 provides the time periods of regime changes which are investigated from the data of EUR–USD. Table B.2 provides the time periods of regime changes which are investigated from the data of GBP–USD.

Table B.1: Time periods of regimes in EUR–USD.

Directional Change: R_{DC}	
Number	Regime 1
1	25/05/2016 10:26:15 – 23/06/2016 17:11:42
2	24/06/2016 13:38:28 – 22/07/2016 04:17:29
Time Series: RV	
1	23/05/2016 – 02/06/2016
2	05/06/2016 – 15/06/2016
3	20/06/2016 – 22/06/2016
4	03/07/2016 – 07/07/2016
5	10/07/2016 – 22/07/2016

Directional Change: R_{DC}	
Number	Regime 2
1	23/06/2016 17:34:21 – 24/06/2016 12:17:02
2	
Time Series: RV	
1	03/06/2016
2	16/06/2016 – 19/06/2016
3	23/06/2016 – 01/07/2016
4	08/07/2016
5	

Table B.2: Time periods of regimes in GBP–USD.

Directional Change: R_{DC}	
Number	Regime 1
1	23/05/2016 04:50:41 − 16/06/2016 03:57:02
2	16/06/2016 04:31:11 − 19/06/2016 19:54:59
3	19/06/2016 23:52:37 − 22/06/2016 17:35:41
4	22/06/2016 21:46:16 − 23/06/2016 06:37:18
5	23/06/2016 10:31:47 − 23/06/2016 16:52:03
6	23/06/2016 17:52:26 − 23/06/2016 19:14:16
7	24/06/2016 05:17:52 − 24/06/2016 06:01:09
8	24/06/2016 07:27:57 − 24/06/2016 08:00:53
9	24/06/2016 12:17
10	24/06/2016 13:31:45 − 24/06/2016 13:48:57
11	24/06/2016 14:32:22 − 24/06/2016 16:51:37
12	26/06/2016 17:59
13	26/06/2016 19:51
14	26/06/2016 21:17:32 − 27/06/2016 05:24:57
15	27/06/2016 07:51:44 − 27/06/2016 09:14:18
16	27/06/2016 10:57:41 − 14/07/2016 07:00:20
17	14/07/2016 08:12:19 − 22/07/2016 04:03:16
Time Series: RV	
1	23/05/2016 − 17/06/2016
2	20/06/2016 − 22/06/2016
3	28/06/2016 − 22/07/2016

Directional Change: R_{DC}	
Number	Regime 2
1	16/06/2016 04:01:58
2	19/06/2016 20:03:54
3	22/06/2016 17:43:58
4	23/06/2016 06:56:43 − 23/06/2016 07:00:53
5	23/06/2016 17:00:43 − 23/06/2016 17:04:06
6	23/06/2016 19:17:56 − 24/06/2016 04:50:48
7	24/06/2016 06:40:44 − 24/06/2016 06:50:23
8	24/06/2016 08:12:47 − 24/06/2016 11:36:15
9	24/06/2016 12:57:35 − 24/06/2016 13:09:33
10	24/06/2016 13:54:30 − 24/06/2016 14:10:50
11	24/06/2016 16:54
12	26/06/2016 18:02:22 − 26/06/2016 18:11:21
13	26/06/2016 19:57
14	27/06/2016 05:35:23 − 27/06/2016 06:05:08
15	27/06/2016 09:19:59 − 27/06/2016 09:35:18
16	14/07/2016 07:03:12 − 14/07/2016 07:09:12
17	
Time Series: RV	
1	19/06/2016
2	23/06/2016 − 27/06/2016
3	

Experiment Summary of Chapter 4

In this appendix, we provided summaries of the experiments of the 10 data sets that were investigated in Chapter 4. For each data set, the information of the experiment is provided, which include the chosen time period, the collected frequency, the major market events that related to the chosen data, the time of the event that took place, the threshold that used to summarise the financial data into DC trends and the timing of the estimated regime changes.

As mentioned in Section 4.3, ten evenly distributed thresholds were applied to summarise the financial data. Here, for each data set, a summary of using one threshold is presented in Tables C.1 through C.10.

Table C.1: Experiment summary of the data of the DJIA.

Data	Dow Jones Industrial Average (DJIA)
Time period	03/01/2007 – 28/12/2012
Data type	Daily closing price
Major market event	Global financial crisis
Timing of the event	The investment bank Lehman Brothers collapsed on 15 September 2008.
Thresholds	0.3%

Time Periods of Regimes	
Regime 1	Regime 2
05/01/2007 – 05/03/2008	10/03/2008 – 01/04/2008
09/04/2008 – 15/07/2008	23/07/2008 – 02/06/2009
03/06/2009 – 26/04/2010	27/04/2010 – 07/06/2010
08/06/2010 – 05/08/2011	08/08/2011 – 14/12/2011
15/12/2011 – 20/12/2012	

Table C.2: Experiment summary of the data of the FTSE 100 Index.

Data	FTSE 100 Index
Time period	02/01/2007 – 31/12/2012
Data type	Daily closing price
Major market event	Global financial crisis
Timing of the event	The investment bank Lehman Brothers collapsed on 15 September 2008.
Thresholds	0.3%

Time Periods of Regimes	
Regime 1	Regime 2
10/01/2007 – 23/07/2007	30/07/2007 – 19/09/2007
20/09/2007 – 14/11/2007	19/11/2007 – 25/03/2008
26/03/2008 – 25/06/2008	26/06/2008 – 13/05/2009
14/05/2009 – 29/04/2010	07/05/2010 – 27/05/2010
02/06/2010 – 22/07/2011	08/08/2011 – 14/12/2011
15/12/2011 – 19/12/2012	15/12/2011 – 19/12/2012

Table C.3: Experiment summary of the data of the S&P 500 Index.

Data	S&P 500 Index
Time period	03/01/2007 – 28/12/2012
Data type	Daily closing price
Major market event	Global financial crisis
Timing of the event	The investment bank Lehman Brothers collapsed on 15 September 2008.
Thresholds	0.3%

Time Periods of Regimes	
Regime 1	Regime 2
05/01/2007 – 05/03/2008	10/03/2008 – 28/03/2008
07/04/2008 – 07/07/2008	08/07/2008 – 03/06/2009
04/06/2009 – 23/04/2010	27/04/2010 – 26/07/2010
29/07/2010 – 03/08/2011	08/08/2011 – 14/12/2011
16/12/2011 – 20/12/2012	

Table C.4: Experiment summary of the data of Brent Crude Oil.

Data	Brent Crude Oil
Time period	02/01/2014 – 30/12/2016
Data type	Daily closing price
Major market event	The collapse of oil prices.
Timing of the event	2014 – 2016
Thresholds	0.3%

Time Periods of Regimes	
Regime 1	Regime 2
03/01/2014 – 03/11/2014	04/11/2014
05/11/2014 – 07/11/2014	17/11/2014 – 01/12/2014
02/12/2014	08/12/2014
09/12/2014	10/12/2014
11/12/2014	22/12/2014 – 07/01/2015
08/01/2015	13/01/2015 – 15/01/2015
22/01/2015 – 29/01/2015	09/02/2015 – 23/02/2015
24/02/2015 – 25/02/2015	27/02/2015 – 02/03/2015
03/03/2015	04/03/2015 – 10/03/2015
12/03/2015	16/03/2015
20/03/2015 – 24/03/2015	26/03/2015 – 24/04/2015
28/04/2015	06/05/2015 – 15/05/2015
18/05/2015	19/05/2015 – 29/05/2015
01/06/2015 – 02/06/2015	04/06/2015 – 16/06/2015
18/06/2015	19/06/2015 – 09/07/2015
21/07/2015 – 29/07/2015	07/08/2015 – 18/09/2015
21/09/2015	22/09/2015 – 24/09/2015
25/09/2015	28/09/2015 – 29/09/2015
30/09/2015 – 01/10/2015	02/10/2015 – 23/10/2015
26/10/2015	27/10/2015 – 29/10/2015
04/11/2015 – 05/11/2015	09/11/2015 – 13/01/2016
14/01/2016	20/01/2016 – 29/02/2016
01/03/2016	02/03/2016 – 12/04/2016
13/04/2016 – 14/04/2016	15/04/2016 – 26/05/2016
27/05/2016 – 03/06/2016	08/06/2016 – 20/06/2016
21/06/2016 – 23/06/2016	27/06/2016 – 29/06/2016
01/07/2016 – 04/07/2016	05/07/2016
07/07/2016	11/07/2016 – 18/07/2016
20/07/2016	02/08/2016 – 14/09/2016
15/09/2016 – 16/09/2016	19/09/2016 – 26/10/2016
27/10/2016	07/11/2016 – 25/11/2016
28/11/2016	29/11/2016 – 21/12/2016

Table C.5: Experiment summary of the data of WTI Crude Oil.

Data	West Texas Intermediate (WTI) Crude Oil
Time period	02/01/2014–30/12/2016
Data type	Daily closing price
Major market event	The collapse of oil prices.
Timing of the event	2014–2016
Thresholds	0.3%

Time Periods of Regimes	
Regime 1	Regime 2
09/01/2014–14/08/2014	15/08/2014–28/12/2016

Table C.6: Experiment summary of the data of the EUR–GBP.

Data	EUR–GBP
Time period	02/05/2016–01/09/2016
Data type	Minute-by-minute
Major market event	UK's EU referendum
Timing of the event	23 June 2016
Thresholds	0.3%

Time Periods of Regimes	
Regime 1	Regime 2
02/05/2016 08:05–23/06/2016 21:51	23/06/2016 21:54–24/06/2016 21:58
26/06/2016 22:54–31/08/2016 15:41	26/06/2016 22:54–31/08/2016 15:41

Table C.7: Experiment summary of the data of the GBP–USD.

Data	GBP–USD
Time period	02/05/2016–01/09/2016
Data type	Minute-by-minute
Major market event	UK's EU referendum
Timing of the event	23 June 2016
Thresholds	0.3%

Time Periods of Regimes	
Regime 1	Regime 2
02/05/2016 13:15 – 23/06/2016 21:51	23/06/2016 22:00 – 28/06/2016 02:53
28/06/2016 03:48 – 14/07/2016 11:58	14/07/2016 12:00 – 14/07/2016 13:04
14/07/2016 14:44 – 31/08/2016 14:33	14/07/2016 14:44 – 31/08/2016 14:33

Table C.8: Experiment summary of the data of the EUR–USD.

Data	EUR–USD
Time period	02/05/2016 – 01/09/2016
Data type	Minute-by-minute
Major market event	UK's EU referendum
Timing of the event	23 June, 2016
Thresholds	0.3%

Time Periods of Regimes	
Regime 1	Regime 2
03/05/2016 09:10 – 23/06/2016 22:15	23/06/2016 22:35 – 24/06/2016 18:34
26/06/2016 21:50 – 31/08/2016 13:48	

Table C.9: Experiment summary of the data of the Shanghai Stock Exchange Composite Index (SSE).

Data	SSE
Time period	06/10/2014 – 06/09/2017
Data type	Daily closing price
Major market event	Chinese stock market turbulence
Timing of the event	2015 – 2016
Thresholds	0.3%

Time Periods of Regimes	
Regime 1	Regime 2
10/06/2014 10:15 – 11/11/2014 09:39	11/11/2014 09:46 – 13/11/2014 10:08
13/11/2014 10:38 – 28/11/2014 13:17	28/11/2014 13:40 – 13/01/2015 10:37
13/01/2015 11:07 – 14/01/2015 14:26	14/01/2015 14:32 – 02/02/2015 09:52
02/02/2015 10:23 – 04/02/2015 14:20	04/02/2015 14:28 – 10/02/2015 09:30
10/02/2015 10:42 – 23/03/2015 14:59	24/03/2015 09:34 – 27/03/2015 10:14
27/03/2015 10:31 – 02/04/2015 14:59	03/04/2015 09:30 – 30/04/2015 10:10
30/04/2015 10:29 – 04/05/2015 09:30	04/05/2015 09:34 – 14/05/2015 10:39
14/05/2015 11:16 – 20/05/2015 14:22	20/05/2015 14:40 – 29/09/2015 09:49
29/09/2015 10:29 – 12/10/2015 10:42	12/10/2015 10:47 – 16/11/2015 10:19
16/11/2015 10:35 – 27/11/2015 13:29	27/11/2015 13:33 – 04/12/2015 09:50
04/12/2015 10:06 – 04/01/2016 10:16	04/01/2016 10:20 – 03/02/2016 10:13
03/02/2016 10:37 – 23/02/2016 14:07	23/02/2016 14:20 – 14/03/2016 09:40
14/03/2016 11:10 – 20/04/2016 09:30	20/04/2016 13:10 – 21/04/2016 10:02
21/04/2016 10:18 – 27/07/2016 10:10	27/07/2016 13:16 – 28/07/2016 09:48
28/07/2016 10:02 – 09/06/2017 10:25	

Table C.10: Experiment summary of the data of the Shenzhen Stock Exchange Component Index (SZSE).

Data	SZSE
Time period	06/10/2014 – 06/09/2017
Data type	Daily closing price
Major market event	Chinese stock market turbulence
Timing of the event	2015 – 2016
Thresholds	0.3%

Time Periods of Regimes	
Regime 1	Regime 2
10/06/2014 09:34 – 17/09/2014 15:00	18/09/2014 09:31 – 18/09/2014 09:51
18/09/2014 10:03 – 28/11/2014 13:41	28/11/2014 14:07 – 31/12/2014 10:11
31/12/2014 10:30 – 05/01/2015 09:50	05/01/2015 09:55 – 14/01/2015 10:02
14/01/2015 10:49 – 16/01/2015 15:00	19/01/2015 09:57 – 22/01/2015 10:00
22/01/2015 10:22 – 23/01/2015 11:23	23/01/2015 13:00 – 03/02/2015 09:41
03/02/2015 09:59 – 04/02/2015 14:20	04/02/2015 14:24 – 09/02/2015 10:11
09/02/2015 10:32 – 20/03/2015 11:24	20/03/2015 13:38 – 23/03/2015 10:07
23/03/2015 10:43 – 24/03/2015 09:30	24/03/2015 09:33 – 27/03/2015 10:12
27/03/2015 10:31 – 30/03/2015 14:44	30/03/2015 14:51 – 02/04/2015 11:26
02/04/2015 13:17 – 08/04/2015 09:30	08/04/2015 09:37 – 10/04/2015 10:12
10/04/2015 10:36 – 13/04/2015 14:39	14/04/2015 09:32 – 29/04/2015 09:52
29/04/2015 10:38 – 04/05/2015 09:30	04/05/2015 09:34 – 04/05/2015 09:48
04/05/2015 10:34 – 05/05/2015 10:48	05/05/2015 11:19 – 18/05/2015 10:38
18/05/2015 13:41 – 20/05/2015 14:22	20/05/2015 14:40 – 11/06/2015 10:30
11/06/2015 10:51 – 12/06/2015 14:05	12/06/2015 14:14 – 30/09/2015 10:48
30/09/2015 13:32 – 08/10/2015 09:30	08/10/2015 09:32 – 08/10/2015 09:49
08/10/2015 10:03 – 12/10/2015 11:25	12/10/2015 13:17 – 19/11/2015 10:13
19/11/2015 10:38 – 23/11/2015 13:53	23/11/2015 14:09 – 24/11/2015 10:09
24/11/2015 10:44 – 26/11/2015 14:18	26/11/2015 14:29 – 14/12/2015 09:49
14/12/2015 10:13 – 28/12/2015 13:19	28/12/2015 13:23 – 29/12/2015 10:08
29/12/2015 10:23 – 04/01/2016 09:50	04/01/2016 09:55 – 03/02/2016 10:49
03/02/2016 11:21 – 24/02/2016 15:00	25/02/2016 10:03 – 16/03/2016 10:49
16/03/2016 11:00 – 23/03/2016 14:01	23/03/2016 14:21 – 25/03/2016 10:02
25/03/2016 10:30 – 20/04/2016 10:25	20/04/2016 11:17 – 21/04/2016 10:01
21/04/2016 10:18 – 06/05/2016 11:10	06/05/2016 11:19 – 10/05/2016 09:50
10/05/2016 10:15 – 13/06/2016 14:09	13/06/2016 14:16 – 14/06/2016 09:54
14/06/2016 10:24 – 24/06/2016 09:30	24/06/2016 09:46 – 27/06/2016 09:47
27/06/2016 13:32 – 27/07/2016 13:01	27/07/2016 13:05 – 28/07/2016 13:31
28/07/2016 13:52 – 09/06/2017 10:38	

Detected Regime Changes in Chapter 4

In this appendix, we present the timeline graph of the detected regime changes for the chosen data set in Chapter 4. As discussed in Section 4.3.2, we have used ten thresholds for each data set in Chapter 4. Here, we present Figure D.1 through D.10 for a representative threshold only (namely 0.003).

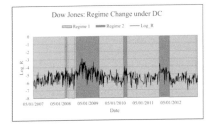

FIGURE D.1: Detected regime changes in the Dow Jones Index.

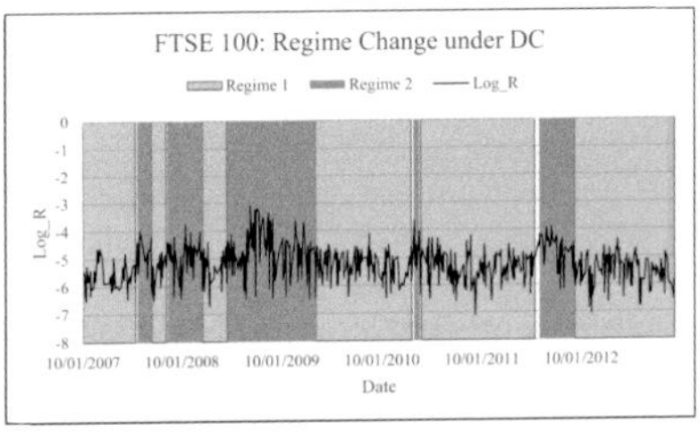

FIGURE D.2: Detected regime changes in the FTSE 100 Index.

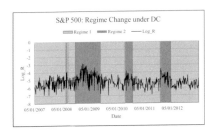

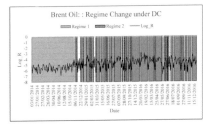

FIGURE D.3: Detected regime changes in the S&P 500 Index.

FIGURE D.4: Detected regime changes in Brent Oil.

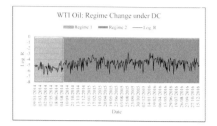

FIGURE D.5: Detected regime changes in WTI Oil.

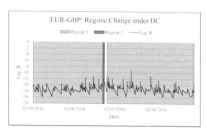

FIGURE D.6: Detected regime changes in EUR–GBP.

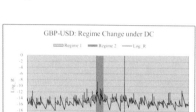

FIGURE D.7: Detected regime changes in GBP–USD.

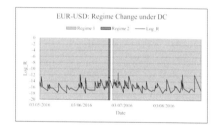

FIGURE D.8: Detected regime changes in EUR–USD.

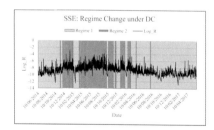

FIGURE D.9: Detected regime changes in the SSE Index.

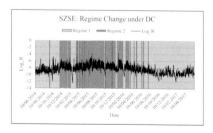

FIGURE D.10: Detected regime changes in the SZSE Index.

Bibliography

[1] Monetary policy summary and minutes of the monetary policy committee meeting ending on 13 July 2016. Bank of England, https://www.bankofengland.co.uk/-/media/boe/files/mo netary-policy-summary-and-minutes/2016/july-2016.pdf. [Online; Publication date: 14 July 2016].

[2] Selim Aksoy and Robert M Haralick. Feature normalization and likelihood-based similarity measures for image retrieval. *Pattern recognition letters*, 22(5):563–582, 2001.

[3] Monira Aloud and Maria Fasli. Exploring trading strategies and their effects in the foreign exchange market. *Computational Intelligence*, 33(2):280–307, 2017.

[4] Monira Aloud, Maria Fasli, Edward Tsang, Alexandre Dupuis, and Richard Olsen. Stylized facts of the fx market transactions data: An empirical study. *Journal of Finance and Investment Analysis*, 2(4):145–183, 2013.

[5] Monira Aloud, Edward PK Tsang, Richard Olsen, and Alexandre Dupuis. A directional-change events approach for studying financial time series. *Economics Discussion Paper*, (2011–28), 2011.

[6] Ethem Alpaydin. *Introduction to machine learning*. MIT Press, 2014.

[7] Andrew Ang and Geert Bekaert. How regimes affect asset allocation. *Financial Analysts Journal*, 60(2):86–99, 2004.

[8] Andrew Ang and Allan Timmermann. Regime changes and financial markets. *Annu. Rev. Financ. Econ.*, 4(1):313–337, 2012.

[9] Han Ao. *A Directional Changes based study on stock market*. PhD thesis, Centre for Computational Finance and Economic Agents (CCFEA), University of Essex, 2018.

[10] Caroline Bain. *Guide to Commodities: Producers, players and prices, markets, consumers and trends.* John Wiley & Sons, 2013.

[11] Amer Bakhach. *Developing trading strategies under the Directional Changes framework, with application in the FX market.* PhD thesis, Centre for Computational Finance and Economic Agents (CCFEA), University of Essex, 2018.

[12] Amer Bakhach, Venkata Chinthalapati, Edward Tsang, and Abdul El Sayed. Intelligent dynamic backlash agent: A trading strategy based on the directional change framework. *Algorithms,* 11(11):171, 2018.

[13] Amer Bakhach, Edward PK Tsang, and Hamid Jalalian. Forecasting directional changes in the FX markets. *2016 IEEE Symposium Series on Computational Intelligence (SSCI),* pages 1–8, 2016.

[14] Amer M Bakhach, Edward PK Tsang, and VL Raju Chinthalapati. Tsfdc: A trading strategy based on forecasting directional change. *Intelligent Systems in Accounting, Finance and Management,* 2018.

[15] Leonard E Baum and Ted Petrie. Statistical inference for probabilistic functions of finite state Markov chains. *The annals of mathematical statistics,* 37(6):1554–1563, 1966.

[16] Thomas Bayes, Richard Price, and John Canton. An essay towards solving a problem in the doctrine of chances. 1763. *MD computing: computers in medical practice,* 8(3):157, 1991.

[17] T Bisig, A Dupuis, V Impagliazzo, and RB Olsen. The scale of market quakes. *Quantitative Finance,* 12(4):501–508, 2012.

[18] William A Branch and George W Evans. Asset return dynamics and learning. *The Review of Financial Studies,* 23(4):1651–1680, 2010.

[19] Jun Chen and Edward PK Tsang. Classification of normal and abnormal regimes in financial markets. *Algorithms,* 11(12):202, 2018.

[20] Michel M Dacorogna, Ramazan Gençay, Ulrich Müller, Richard B Olsen, and Pictet Olivier V. *An introduction to high-frequency finance.* Elsevier, 2001.

[21] Qiang Dai, Kenneth J Singleton, and Wei Yang. Is regime-shift risk priced in the US treasury market? Working paper, New York University and Stanford University, 2003.

[22] Gavyn Davies. Regime changes in the financial markets. *Financial Times*, https://www.ft.com/content/6556ec60-6aa3-3dfe-8953-b94d6080c360, 2016. [Online].

[23] Rene Garcia, Richard Luger, and Eric Renault. Empirical assessment of an intertemporal option pricing model with latent variables. *Journal of Econometrics*, 116(1–2):49–83, 2003.

[24] Amitabha Ghosh. Scaling laws. In *Mechanics over micro and nano scales*, pages 61–94. Springer, 2011.

[25] Eric Ghysels. On the periodic structure of the business cycle. *Journal of Business & Economic Statistics*, 12(3):289–298, 1994.

[26] Chris Giles. Bank of england holds interest rates despite brexit concerns. *Financial Times*, https://www.ft.com/content/1b1e0b0e-49b3-11e6-b387-64ab0a67014c, 2016. [Online].

[27] James B Glattfelder, A Dupuis, and Richard B Olsen. Patterns in high-frequency fx data: discovery of 12 empirical scaling laws. *Quantitative Finance*, 11(4):599–614, 2011.

[28] Anton Golub, James B Glattfelder, and Richard B Olsen. The alpha engine: Designing an automated trading algorithm. In *High-Performance Computing in Finance*, pages 49–76. Chapman & Hall/CRC Series in Mathematical Finance, 2018.

[29] Dominique M Guillaume, Michel M Dacorogna, Rakhal R Davé, Ulrich A Müller, Richard B Olsen, and Olivier V Pictet. From the bird's eye to the microscope: A survey of new stylized facts of the intra-daily foreign exchange markets. *Finance and stochastics*, 1(2):95–129, 1997.

[30] James D Hamilton. A new approach to the economic analysis of nonstationary time series and the business cycle. *Econometrica: Journal of the Econometric Society*, pages 357–384, 1989.

[31] James D Hamilton. Regime switching models. In *Macroeconometrics and time series analysis*, pages 202–209. Springer, 2010.

[32] James D Hamilton. Macroeconomic regimes and regime shifts. In *Handbook of macroeconomics*, volume 2, pages 163–201. Elsevier, 2016.

[33] Daniel Jurafsky and H. James Martin. *Speech and Language Processing: An Introduction to Natural Language Processing, Computational Linguistics, and Speech Recognition.* Prentice Hall, 2018.

[34] Mark Kritzman, Sebastien Page, and David Turkington. Regime shifts: Implications for dynamic strategies (corrected). *Financial Analysts Journal*, 68(3):22–39, 2012.

[35] K Ming Leung. Naive bayesian classifier. *Polytechnic University Department of Computer Science/Finance and Risk Engineering*, 2007.

[36] Katie Martin and Michael Hunter. Pound and gilts at epicentre as brexit fears shake markets. `https://www.ft.com/content/8`
`72ddbfa-3133-11e6-bda0-04585c31b153`, 2016. [Online].

[37] Shaimaa Hussein Masry. *Event-Based Microscopic Analysis of the FX Market.* PhD thesis, Centre for Computational Finance and Economic Agents (CCFEA), University of Essex.

[38] George Parker, Michael Mackenzie, and Ben Hall. Britain turns its back on Europe. `https://www.ft.com/content/e404c2fc-`
`3913-11e6-9a05-82a9b15a8ee7`, 2016. [Online].

[39] Jeremy Piger. Econometrics: Models of regime changes. In *Encyclopedia of Complexity and Systems Science*, pages 2744–2757. Springer, 2009.

[40] Lawrence R Rabiner. A tutorial on hidden Markov models and selected applications in speech recognition. *Proceedings of the IEEE*, 77(2):257–286, 1989.

[41] Irina Rish et al. An empirical study of the naive Bayes classifier. In *IJCAI 2001 workshop on empirical methods in artificial intelligence*, volume 3, pages 41–46, 2001.

[42] Hazel Sheffield. Pound sterling rises against the dollar as Theresa May becomes prime minister. *The Independent*, `http://www.in`
`dependent.co.uk/news/business/news/pound-sterling-ther`

`esa-may-prime-minister-ftse-100-brexit-eu-referendum`
`-a7133991.html`, 2016. [Online].

[43] Arthur Sklarew. *Techniques of a professional commodity chart analyst.* Commodity Research Bureau, 1980.

[44] Edward PK Tsang. Directional changes, definitions. Working Paper, WP050-10, Centre for Computational Finance and Economic Agents (CCFEA), University of Essex, 2010.

[45] Edward PK Tsang. Directional changes: A new way to look at price dynamics. *International Conference on Computational Intelligence, Communications, and Business Analytics*, pages 45–55, 2017.

[46] Edward PK Tsang and Jun Chen. Regime change detection using directional change indicators in the foreign exchange market to chart Brexit. *IEEE Transactions in Emerging Technology in Computational Intelligence (TETCI)*, 2(3):185–193, 2018.

[47] Edward PK Tsang, Ran Tao, Antoaneta Serguieva, and Shuai Ma. Profiling high-frequency equity price movements in directional changes. *Quantitative finance*, 17(2):217–225, 2017.

[48] Ruey S Tsay. *Analysis of Financial Time Series, 3rd Edition.* John Wiley & Sons, Inc., 2012.

[49] Johan Van Benthem. *The logic of time: a model-theoretic investigation into the varieties of temporal ontology and temporal discourse.* D Reidel Publishing Co, 1983.

[50] Paul Virilio and Sylvère Lotringer. *Pure War.* The MIT Press, 2008.

[51] Ingmar Visser and Maarten Speekenbrink. depmixs4: An r-package for hidden Markov models. *Journal of Statistical Software*, 36(7):1–21, 2010.

Index